how to pl@y
internet
poker
«to win»

how to pl@y internet poker «to win»

victor knight

foulsham

LONDON • NEW YORK • TORONTO • SYDNEY

foulsham

The Publishing House, Bennetts Close, Cippenham, Slough, Berkshire, SL1 5AP, England

Foulsham books can be found in all good bookshops and direct from www.foulsham.com

ISBN 13: 978-0-572-03181-7
ISBN 10: 0-572-03181-5

A CIP record for this book is available from the British Library

Printed in China through Colorcraft Ltd.,HK

Contents

Introduction

Although the origins of real-life poker are largely unknown, there is little doubt that it is easily the world's most popular card game. Now played all around the globe, it is thought that it may have been first imported to the US from France during the nineteenth century and could be a direct descendant of the Persian game Âs Nas.

The first direct references to poker can be found in newspapers from New Orleans dated around 1830. From New Orleans the game then spread rapidly up the Mississippi River on the famous steamboats, and also across to the east of the country via the new railways which were just coming into use. But it was when it hit the Wild West that poker really boomed in popularity, spawning tales of games between legendary figures from the new frontier. Indeed, Wild Bill Hickock reputedly met his death during a game while clutching a hand of Aces and 8s – a set of cards that quickly became known as 'Dead Man's Hand'.

How ironic then that in the late 1990s poker spread like wildfire across another new frontier, but one that was this time purely electronic. That new frontier was the internet.

PlanetPoker was the first company to offer an online poker room, with Paradise Poker following not far behind. Thanks to sites like these a huge industry was created. From its launch date in September 1999 through to April 2002, Paradise Poker reportedly dealt over 177,000,000 hands – yes, 177 million! Given a modest rake (the amount site operators take from each pot) of just 50 US cents, that was an enormous amount of revenue. No wonder then that more sites came online.

By early 2001, industry experts had put the number of online poker players at 5000 a day. But compared to now that figure pales into insignificance. Today, one site alone, PartyPoker (the world's biggest), can sometimes boast of up to 30,000 players at any one time.

There can be no doubt that online poker was a tremendously inventive use of the internet and has made a lot of money for those who first thought of the idea. But there is nothing wrong with that. After all, the online version of the game has now become an easily accessible recreational pursuit for millions of people worldwide. The sheer variety in background of those who play internet poker is quite startling. As a snapshot, one evening late in August 2005 PartyPoker could boast of players from the UK, US, Australia, Iceland,

Germany, Estonia, Brazil, Mexico, Poland, India, France, Spain, Argentina and Ireland. A quick dip into some of the games, using the facility of the text-box – which allows players to communicate with one another – revealed that the occupations of those playing included doctor, firefighter, shopkeeper, businessman, tree surgeon, writer, builder and insurance clerk.

For anyone wondering about the type of people who play poker online, this snapshot gives the answer. Quite simply, people from all backgrounds, races and financial standing log on and enjoy the game. This is not least of all because the different sites offer a tremendous range of games and tables, with stakes starting from as little as a few pence.

The other reason that online poker continues to gain in popularity is because it is very easy to play. At any one time most of the sites offer a number of different versions of the game, including Texas Hold 'em, Omaha Hold 'em, Seven-card Stud and others. However, the first on that list, Texas Hold 'em, is by far and away the most popular. This is not only due to the fact that it is so simple to play but also because it offers so much scope for betting action.

The betting action is crucial to poker because without it the game would be pretty pointless. All levels of stakes are accommodated in online games, from a few pence through to thousands of pounds. As you might expect, the amount that can be won is dependent upon the size of stakes being played with, but even at the lower levels a player who enjoys a good run of cards, and who knows how to play them, can still walk away with a healthy profit.

It is important to stress, though, that to make a consistent profit from online poker, a complete beginner must approach the game with a reasonable enough knowledge of it to play their cards intelligently. Hence this book.

The book has been written with the specific purpose of taking someone who has never logged into an online poker game through the basics of how to play (Texas Hold 'em in particular), how to log into a site, how to find plenty of play-money practice games (absolutely essential), winning techniques for the real-money tables, managing a bankroll, managing table stakes, and even managing the mood swings that the game of poker brings to almost every player.

But the book is not only designed to appeal to complete newcomers. No, it will also serve well the needs of those players who have only recently discovered the game but have not yet become practised at it. In short, it should be of enormous help in turning newcomers and novices alike into winning players.

So, let's get started. Deal those cards!

The Most Popular Games

Poker, whether it is played in real life or on the internet, takes many forms. Fortunately though, the concept of the game remains the same no matter what version is being used. This is good because it means that once a newcomer has learned the basics they will quickly be able to master all the different ways it is played.

On the internet by far the most popular version of the game is Texas Hold 'em. The structure of Texas Hold 'em allows for plenty of betting action, hence its popularity, and it is also very easy to understand. However, despite the huge appeal of Texas Hold 'em the vast majority of internet poker sites also offer Omaha Hold 'em (the normal and the hi / lo version) and Seven-card Stud. Some sites offer even more versions than these but they are not in wide enough use to justify mentioning in this book.

Whatever the version of the game, almost all internet poker site operators offer the facility to play in ring games or in tournaments. Ring games are where the players compete for real money (represented by chips) against one another, while tournaments still see the participants competing against each other, but for make-believe money (again represented by chips). These chips are obtained through paying an entry fee for the tournament.

In a tournament, players are eliminated once they have run out of chips, with usually the last three left in winning varying degrees of prize money, this prize money having been made up from the entry fees of everyone who entered the tournament. Naturally, the overall winner of a tournament will be the player who has won the chips off everyone else.

The higher the entry fee for a tournament, the bigger the prize money will normally be, with some tournaments offering huge rewards either through carrying steep entry fees or because they are set up for a very large number of players. However, at this stage there is no need to worry about ring games or tournaments because we will return to them later on in the book. For now, let's go through the very basics of poker before then looking to see how the most popular versions of it are played.

Five Cards

No matter what version of the game is being played, or whether it is being played in real life or online, a poker hand consists of five cards. Depending upon the version, a hand can be composed from a varying number of cards, but this is something which will become clear when we examine the different games. To start with, all you need to remember is that a poker hand consists of five cards.

Each hand in poker is ranked in order of value. That value is dictated by the probability of the hand being dealt direct from a 52-card deck. The hand which carries the lowest probability of being obtained is the most valuable and the rest are then ranked in descending order depending upon their probability of being dealt straight from the pack. Note that the different suits in a deck all carry equal value; in other words, none are ranked higher than the others. There are nine ranked hands in poker, each with a highest and lowest possible make-up. Let's take a look at them in descending order.

Number 1: Straight Flush (40 combinations)

Highest make-up (also known as a royal flush):

Lowest make-up:

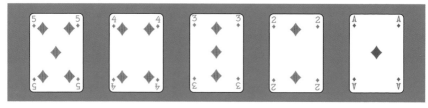

Description: Five cards of the same suit in sequence. Between two or more straight flushes, the highest-ranking top card wins. A tie is possible.

Probability of being dealt this hand straight from the deck: 0.0015% or 1 in 64,974

Number 2: Four of a Kind (624 combinations)

Highest make-up:

Lowest make-up:

Description: Four cards of the same rank, with an odd fifth card. Between two similar hands, the one with the higher-ranking four cards will win. There cannot be a tie so the fifth card is of no consequence. **Probability** of being dealt this hand straight from the deck: 0.0024% or 1 in 4165

Number 3: Full House (3744 combinations)

Highest make-up:

Lowest make-up:

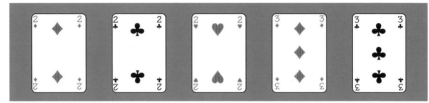

Description: Three cards of one rank (a triple) with two of another (a pair). Between two full houses, the one with the higher-ranking set of three wins. Ties are impossible.

Probability of being dealt this hand straight from the deck: 0.1441% or 1 in 694

Number 4: Flush (5108 combinations)

Highest make-up:

Lowest make-up:

Description: Five cards of the same suit, but not in sequence. Between flushes, the one containing the highest card wins. If equal, the second highest wins, and so on. Ties possible.

Probability of being dealt this hand straight from the deck: 0.1967% or 1 in 509

Number 5: Straight (10,200 combinations)

Highest make-up:

Lowest make-up:

Description: Five cards in sequence, but not of the same suit. Between straights, the one containing the highest card at the top of the sequence wins. Note that A, K, Q, J, 10 beats 5, 4, 3, 2, A where the Ace counts low. Ties possible.

Probability of being dealt this hand straight from the deck: 0.3925% or 1 in 255

Number 6: Three of a Kind (54,912 combinations)

Highest make-up:

Lowest make-up:

Description: Three cards of the same rank with two unmatching cards. Between similar hands the one with the highest-ranking three wins. Ties not possible.

Probability of being dealt this hand straight from the deck: 2.1129% or 1 in 47

Number 7: Two Pairs (123,552 combinations)

Highest make-up:

Lowest make-up:

Description: Two cards of one rank, two of another and an odd card. Between similar hands the one with the highest-ranking pair wins. If equal, the highest-ranking second pair wins; if still equal, the highest-ranking odd card decides matters. Ties possible.

Probability of being dealt this hand straight from the deck: 4.7539% or 1 in 21

Number 8: One Pair (1,098,240 combinations)

Highest make-up:

Lowest make-up:

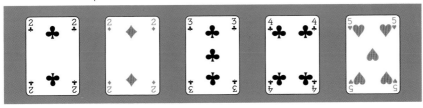

Description: Two cards of one rank, with three unmatching cards. Between similar hands the highest-ranking pair wins. If equal, the highest-ranking odd card wins; if still equal, the next highest-ranking odd card decides matters, and so on. Ties possible.
Probability of being dealt this hand straight from the deck: 42.2569% or 1 in 2.3665

Number 9: Nothing! (1,302,540 combinations)

Highest make-up:

Lowest make-up:

Description: No accepted name for this hand, though often known as 'no-pair' or 'high-card'. Hands of this kind are graded by the highest-ranked card they contain; if equal, by the second highest, and so on. Ties possible.

Probability of being dealt this hand straight from the deck: 50.1177% or 1 in 1.9953

What we have just seen are the nine ranking poker hands. No matter what version of the game is being played, these rankings never change. What also never changes is the object of poker.

Object of the Game

The object of poker is to win the money bet into each 'pot'. The pot is the amount of cash bet by each player on each hand. Regardless of whether the game is being played in real life or on the internet, and regardless of what version is being played, there is always a pot. However, the way the pot builds up does vary slightly across the different versions of the game. Hence, for the time being just remember that the pot is the amount of money being competed for.

Ways to Win

Regardless of the version of the game, there are two ways to win a pot at poker:
- Through having the highest hand at the 'showdown'.
- Through being the last player left in and thus no showdown being required.

Let's look briefly at both of these ways.

Once all the cards in a game have been dealt (the actual number depends upon the version of the game being played), and all the betting is complete, providing there is more than one player left in there will be a showdown. At a showdown the player with the highest-ranking hand wins the pot, or the pot is split if the players have identical hands.

Alternatively, if only one player remains in that player will automatically win the pot. A player can be the last one left in a hand for a variety of reasons. The most frequent occurrences are where every other player has surrendered their cards because they have not considered them good enough to continue with, or because they felt the stake money required to stay in the pot was too high, given the cards they held.

These reasons begin to illustrate that there is far more to poker than just the cards each player holds: while the cards are the most crucial factor there is also the way they are played. Here is where poker played in real life begins to differ from that played online. However, this book is about internet poker so we do not need to worry about the ways that real-life players try to bluff and outmanoeuvre one another, although later in the book we will briefly examine these topics as they apply to the online version of the game.

How Poker Works

Most versions of poker are easy to understand, but they can be a little difficult to explain. The problem is that to understand a run-through of a game you need to know the terms being used, but in order to understand the terms being used you need to understand a run-through of a game! It's a bit of a chicken-and-egg situation.

To try to overcome this, what follows is a list of internet poker terms common to most versions of the game. After that will be an outline of a Texas Hold 'em game followed by a run-through of a game in action. Use all three things in conjunction and you should have little trouble quickly grasping how Texas Hold 'em, plus the other versions of poker that follow, works.

Common Terms

Ante: With some versions of poker each player is required to put an amount of money, known as the ante, into the pot before any cards are dealt. This is done so that each pot already has something in it before the players begin to bet on their cards.

Bet: The first player to act in each fresh betting interval will not have the option to 'call' (see below) because nobody will have made a bet before them. Instead they will have the option to bet (or 'check' in certain betting intervals). This simply means putting into the pot any amount they wish and which the betting limits for the game allow.

Betting Intervals: The betting intervals are the periods in the game when the betting takes place. These occur after the players have been dealt first some, then some more, then all of the cards. The number of betting intervals will depend upon the version of poker being played. As you will learn, with Texas Hold 'em there are four betting intervals. A betting interval ends when all the players left in have contributed an equal amount to the pot.

Betting Limits: In games with fixed-limit staking, each player will only be allowed to bet (or 'raise') the amount specified by the limit. So, in a game that is £2 / £4, before the 'turn' card each player will be allowed to bet or raise in £2 increments. After the turn card the limit will increase to £4 – hence the £2 / £4.

Betting Rounds: The betting rounds are when, during each betting interval, all the players have the opportunity to bet at least once. The number of betting rounds which take place is dictated by how long it is before each player has contributed an equal amount to the pot. (Remember that when this has happened the betting interval ends.)

Blind Bets: The 'blinds' are just another form of ante. However, the difference is that the two blinds (called the small and the big) come from just two players. This is opposed to antes, where every player is required to cough up. Don't worry though; the same two players do not have to pay the blinds every hand! No, the obligation to put in the blind bets revolves around the table each deal – something that will become clear shortly.

Call: To put into the pot an amount equal in size to that of the last bet made.

Check: A bet to nothing. Checking is only available from the second betting interval onwards, and then only until a bet has been made. When a player checks, it indicates that they wish to stay in the hand but, at that particular point, not bet any further chips.

Chips: Most people know this already but just in case someone out there thinks we are talking about the potato variety, in casinos and on the internet chips are used to represent the amount of money being bet.

Community Cards: The five cards dealt face-up in the middle of the table which are available to all of the players.

Deal: In poker, and with card games generally, the word 'deal' is used both as a verb and a noun. The deal is another name for each hand but is also used as in 'to deal'.

Dealer: In real-life games played in casinos or card rooms, a dealer is usually provided. This individual will take no part in the game and is there to deal the cards and administer the pot. However, in many real-life games there is no dealer, with the players themselves taking it in turn to perform this duty. With internet games there is always a dealer, but it is electronic. In other words, the site's software will deal the cards and administer the pot. That said, the site software needs to keep track of which player would have been dealer had they been carrying out the task themselves. See the next definition for why this is the case.

Dealer's Disc (or Button): Most versions of poker see the betting sequence begin with the player immediately to the dealer's left. Because the position of the players in the betting is a crucial part of the game (we will see why later), it would ruin things if the same player always had to bet first. Therefore, when a formal dealer is used, be it a real-life or an electronic one, the game proceeds as if the players were taking it in turn to deal themselves. This is achieved through the use of a dealer's disc, or button as it is also known.

Quite simply, on each deal, the disc moves from right to left around the table to show which player would have been dealing had there not been a formal dealer. In this way the betting sequence will always start off from a different position, with all the players being treated equally as a result. Later on when we look at some ways to improve your chances of winning at poker, we will return to the betting positions because they are extremely important.

Fold (or Stack): When a player gives up their hand, they are said to fold (or stack) their cards.

Flop: The first three of the five community cards.

Hand: The cards each player is dealt. However, note that the word 'hand' is also used generically to describe each deal.

Hole-cards: The first two cards dealt face-down to every player.

Pot: The aggregate amount of money bet on each hand.

Raise: To put into the pot an amount greater than the last bet made.

Re-raise: Only applicable when a player sitting immediately to the left of someone who has just made a raise then puts into the pot an amount greater than that raise.

River: The fifth and last of the five community cards.

Showdown: If it is required, the point in a game, regardless of the version being played, where the players who remain in compare their hands.

Stake: The amount of money each player bets into each hand.

Turn: The fourth of the five community cards.

Texas Hold 'em

Texas Hold 'em is easily the most popular version of internet poker, thanks to its simplicity and also to the fact that it allows so much betting action. It can be played by a maximum of ten players with the dealer's disc moving around the table from right to left.

As with all the different versions of poker, a hand is made up of five cards. But how those five cards are obtained is the major variation between the different types of game. This will become clear as we progress.

In looking at how this version of the game is played, we will also see the way the betting associated with it works – remember, without betting, poker would be pretty dreary! Also remember that we will be describing how the game works on the internet as opposed to real life, although there is virtually (excuse the pun) no difference between how the game is played both online and not.

Texas Hold 'em Outline

The objective of each player is to make the best poker hand from the first two cards – which are dealt face-down exclusively to them (known as the **hole-cards**) – plus the five cards dealt face-up, which are available to all the players (these are known as the **community cards**).

Each player can make up their hand using any combination of their two hole-cards and the five community cards. So, they can use one of their hole-cards and four of the community cards, both of their hole-cards and three of the community cards, or all five of the community cards (this is known as playing the board).

The Blinds

Before the hole-cards are dealt, the two players seated immediately to the left and next left of whoever is holding the dealer's disc are required to put in the **small** and **large** blind bets respectively.

The Hole-Cards

Once the two hole-cards have been dealt, each player looks at them. The first player to act will be the one seated to the immediate left of the player who put in the big blind. This player will have the option to **call**, **raise** or **fold**. (Note that they will not be able to **check** as the blind bets will already have been made.)

After the first player has acted, all of the other players take it in turn to do so. Note here that the player who put in the small blind will have to increase their stake even if they just want to call (of course, this is only if they wish to continue in the hand).

Once all the players who have remained in have contributed an equal amount to the pot, the **betting interval** ends. This is known as the stakes being equalised. (The **betting rounds** continue until the stakes are equalised.)

The Flop

From the players left in, after the flop the first to act will be the one seated nearest to the left of the player holding the dealer's disc. This player will have the option to either **bet**, **check** or **fold**.

Again, the betting round will then continue from right to left with each player acting in turn. Remember though, the checking option will not be available once a player has made a bet. Also, after the first bet has been made the subsequent players will not have the bet option; instead this will be replaced by the choice of 'call'. They will also have the further option to raise. Once the pot is equalised, the betting interval will end.

The Turn

The fourth community card, known as the **turn**, will then be dealt. After this the next betting interval will commence with, from those left in, the player again being the one who is seated nearest to the left of the dealer's disc.

As with all the betting intervals, the betting rounds will continue until the stakes of the players have been equalised.

The River

The fifth and last community card to be dealt is called the **river**.

Once the river card is dealt, the final betting interval begins, again kicking off with the player still in who is sitting nearest to the left of the dealer's disc. This time when all the stakes have been equalised, providing there is more than one player still in, a **showdown** will take place with the best hand winning.

A Game in Action

To pull all of this together let's now look at a game in action. There are five players, with the stake limits as follows:

- Small Blind – one chip
- Big Blind – two chips
- Minimum Bet or Raise – three chips
- Maximum Bet or Raise in the first interval – eight chips
- Maximum Bet or Raise in all other intervals – twelve chips

First Betting Interval

Player 1 is holding the dealer's disc, player 2 is the small blind and player 3 the large blind.

1   Player 2 puts in the small blind of **one chip**. Player 3 puts in the big blind of **two chips**.

2   The hole-cards are then dealt, resulting in the following:

Player 1: (dealer)   Player 2: (small blind)

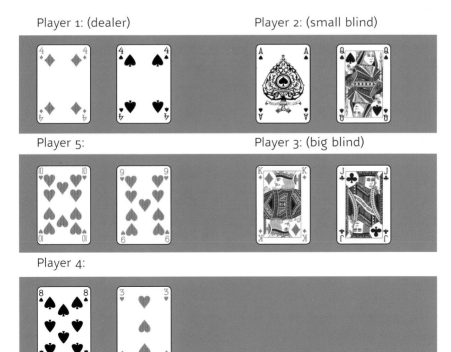

Player 5:   Player 3: (big blind)

Player 4:

3   Player 4 is the first to act (because players 2 and 3 put in the blinds). Player 4 folds because their hole-cards are poor.
4   Player 5 is next and they decide to call the big blind; hence they put **two chips** into the pot.
5   Player 1 thinks that their hole-cards are okay so they call the last blind bet by putting in **two chips**.
6   Player 2 (the small blind) has an excellent set of hole-cards and so they also call through putting in **one chip** (remember, they have already put in one chip for the small blind), but they also decide to raise by putting in **three more chips (four in total)**.
7   Players 3 and 5 decide to call and both put in **three chips** to do so (remember, they had already bet two chips into the pot).
8   Player 1 does the same as the previous two and also puts in **three chips**.

All the players have now put the same amount into the pot and so it is equalised with **20 chips**.

The Flop

The flop cards are dealt and produce the following:

Second Betting Interval

1   Player 2 is now the first required to act. With their hole-card Queen, plus the Queen and the two Jacks which the flop has produced, they have two pairs. Hence they bet **three chips**. (This player could have also checked, which is an option that has now become available.)
2   Player 3 has got three Jacks but decides to call for fear of frightening the other players off if they bet too heavily; therefore they put **three chips** into the pot.
3   Player 4 has already folded.

4   Player 5 decides to stay in because they have two chances of a
    straight. They hold the 9 ♥, 10 ♥ as their hole-cards alongside the
    J ♥, Q ♦ from the flop (either an 8 or a King would give them a
    straight). They also hold three hearts. So if two more came out they
    would have a flush – indeed it would be a straight flush if the Q ♥
    and King ♥ were to appear. As a result, they decide to call and put in
    three chips.
5   Player 1 now holds two pairs (4s and Jacks), but because the Jacks
    belong to all the players they decide to fold.

The pot is now equalised with a total of **29 chips**.

The Turn

The turn card is dealt and produces the following:

Third Betting Interval

1   Player 2 now has the chance of a straight if a King comes out as the
    fifth community card, but they do not feel confident about this and
    decide to check.
2   Player 3 still holds three Jacks but could also make one of two
    straights if either a 9 or an Ace came out as the final community
    card. They decide to bet **ten chips** as a result.
3   Player 5 now holds two pairs (Jacks and 10s) and could also obtain a
    straight if either an 8 or a King came out on the river card. They
    decide to call and put **ten chips** into the pot to do so.
4   Player 1 has already folded.
5   Player 2, who checked to start with, now also decides to call and
    puts in **ten chips**.

The pot is now equalised with **59 chips**.

The River

The river card is now dealt and produces the following:

Fourth Betting Interval

1 Player 2 still holds two pairs, but the river card has done nothing for them. They decide to check.
2 Player 3 now holds a straight, but they also check to see what player 5 will do.
3 Player 5 remains on two pairs, but because they fear these will be beaten they take the chance to stay in at no extra cost through checking.

Because all three players left in have not bet, the pot is still equalised at **59 chips**. The showdown now takes place. This is won by player 3 with the following straight:

So, that is how Texas Hold 'em works. It may seem a bit complicated to begin with, but it does work the same all the time and doesn't take much getting used to. Of course, the beauty of the game is in the way it is actually played – something we look at later on in the book.

You will probably be pleased to know that the other versions of poker we are going to look at are not greatly different from Texas Hold 'em. We'll start with Omaha Hold 'em.

Omaha Hold 'em

Omaha Hold 'em is very similar to Texas Hold 'em, but there are two highly important differences. Although the structure of the game is almost identical, these two differences mean that the game is more complex than Texas Hold 'em. Perhaps this is the reason it is not quite so popular, although it is still widely played.

Explaining the two differences between Omaha Hold 'em and Texas Hold 'em will not take long!

The first difference is that each player receives four hole-cards instead of two. The second is that each player **must** use two of these hole-cards in their final hand (you will recall that with Texas Hold 'em, each player is at liberty to use none, one, or two of their hole-cards).

Other than these two differences, Omaha and Texas Hold 'em both work in the same way, with the betting being identical. However, because four hole-cards are dealt, and because exactly two of them must be used, there is a huge difference in how Omaha is actually played.

In reality, Omaha is considerably more complex than Texas Hold 'em and the ways of playing it are beyond the scope of this book. Suffice to say, anyone thinking of playing this version of poker should make sure they familiarise themselves with its intricacies before doing so.

Before moving away from Omaha, there is one more thing to note. Many internet poker sites see the game played as both 'Omaha' and 'Omaha Hi / Lo'. With the former the highest hand left in wins the pot, but with the latter the pot is shared between the highest and lowest hands. However, to qualify as 'low' the hand must be no better than 8-high (in this instance Aces count only as low). In other words, any hand that does not contain five cards of differing ranks all 8 or lower cannot be used as the low hand. Sometimes this version of the game is known as 'Omaha 8 or better'.

Hi / Lo is an interesting variation of Omaha and there is nothing to stop one player trying to win all the pot by playing two hands at the same time, providing they use exactly two of their hole-cards (the same hole-cards can be used for both a high and a low hand).

Note that each hand will always have a 'high' winner but sometimes there will not be a low enough hand to qualify for a 'low' winner. In such cases, the whole pot will be won by the highest hand. In summary, there are a number of rules with Omaha Hi / Lo which novice players should most definitely read before playing in real-money games.

Seven-Card Stud

A descendant of Five-card Stud (very rarely played online), Seven-card Stud is the third version of poker widely played on the internet. Although the object of the game is still the same as it is with Texas Hold 'em and Omaha (to make the best hand of five cards), Seven-card Stud is played differently. To begin with, there are no blinds. Also, there are no community cards.

Because a hand could see up to seven cards being dealt to each player, seven is the maximum number of players that can play in any one hand.

Let's take a look at a hand of Seven-card Stud in action. To begin, each player puts into the pot an 'ante', as opposed to two players putting up the 'blinds'. This ante will be the same amount for every player. After each player has put in their ante, the game then runs as follows.

Round 1

Each player is dealt two cards face-down and one card face-up. This face-up card is known as the 'door card', or 'third street'. The first round of betting action is then initiated through the player with the lowest door card having to place a bet into the pot, called a 'bring-in' bet. When two or more players have the same lowest card, the player who must make the bring-in bet is determined by suit order, progressing upwards through clubs, diamonds, hearts and spades.

After the bring-in bet, each player calls, raises or folds in turn until all the stakes are equalised. Note that on every betting round, each player is limited to one bet and three raises (four 'bets' in total).

Round 2

Once the stakes in round 1 have been equalised, a second face-up card is dealt to each of the players who remain in the hand. This card is known as 'fourth street'. After this card has been dealt, and also for the rest of the action, the player who has to act first is the one who is currently showing the highest hand on their face-up cards. The betting then continues, going from right to left.

The first player to act will have the option to fold, check or bet. Subsequent players will have the same options until the first bet has been made when, similar to Texas Hold 'em, the option to check will be removed. Once all the bets have been equalised, the round ends.

Round 3

A third face-up card will then be dealt to each of the players. This is commonly known as 'fifth street'. In this round the betting limits double from the previous two rounds. Again, the highest set of face-up cards dictates which player begins the betting. As with the previous rounds, and all subsequent rounds, the option to check will only be available until the first bet is made. Once all the bets are equalised, a further face-up card is dealt to all the players; this card is known as 'sixth street'. This signifies the start of the next round.

Round 4

Once the sixth street card has been dealt, the betting starts again. As with previous rounds, the player with the highest set of face-up cards starts things off. Again, once all the stakes have been equalised, this round of betting ends.

Round 5

The final card is then dealt, known as the 'river', or 'seventh street'. However, note that this card is dealt face-down. A final set of betting then takes place.

The Showdown

As with Texas Hold 'em, any players who are left in progress through to the showdown where the highest hand wins.

Just like Texas Hold 'em, Seven-card Stud is an easy game to learn but far from an easy one to master! There is also a version of Seven-card Stud which many online casinos play called 'Seven-card Stud Hi / Lo'.

2

Betting Limits, Ring Games and Tournaments

B etting is the most important part of poker, be it the online version of the game or in real life. Indeed, without betting the game would be pointless; so in this chapter we take a look at how betting limits work and how the stakes differ in ring games and tournaments.

Stakes

Having looked in chapter 1 at how the three most popular versions of internet poker work, we now need to examine the different staking limits attached to them.

Texas Hold 'em / Omaha / Seven-Card Stud

All these versions of poker can be played as fixed-limit (or limit as it is usually called), pot-limit or no-limit. However, note that the small and large blind bets are still required with Texas Hold 'em and Omaha (antes are required with Seven-card Stud) no matter what stake limit applies to the game. Because, though, it is now the intention of this book to concentrate upon Texas Hold 'em (being far and away the most popular version of online poker), we will examine the staking limits using that as the example.

Fixed-Limit

When poker is played with fixed limits it simply means that every player is only allowed to bet (or raise) the amount specified by that limit each time the action comes to them.

Let's suppose that a fixed-limit game is £2 / £4. This means that before the flop each player can bet £2 or raise £2 (if they raised £2, they would need to put £4 in the pot).

After a raise the next player can either call the raise (in our example that would be £4) or raise by that amount (meaning £8 would be their contribution to the pot). Should there be a raise in this way, the next player could either call it with £8, or make a further raise by putting £16 into the pot. In this way, even with limit games the pots can still build to quite healthy amounts.

However, note that to stop stakes spiralling away there is usually a restriction on the number of bets allowed in any one round (normally one bet and three raises, or one bet and four raises).

On the flop, the betting remains the same, but on the turn and river cards the limits increase. Using our £2 / £4 example, the limits would go up to £4 as a bet or raise and then all bets, calls and raises after that would be in £4 increments.

So, in limit poker the figures stated for the game, in our example £2 / £4, show what the bet and raise increments are up to when the turn card is dealt (left-hand figure – £2) and then what they are for the rest of the hand (right-hand figure – £4).

Fixed-limit games are the safest ones for newcomers to start off with. On most internet poker sites there are plenty of fixed-limit games where the limits are very low – as little as 10p / 20p on some sites.

A final thing to note about fixed-limit games – and this applies to pot-limit and no-limit as well – is that a player will always be restricted to how much they can bet by the amount of money they have on the table in front of them (table stakes). Should the situation occur where a player does not have enough money to call a previous bet, they will have to go 'all-in' if they wish to continue. We'll look at what all-in means shortly.

Pot-Limit

The next level up from fixed-limit games are pot-limit ones. As the name suggests, in this type of game, players are allowed to bet any amount up to, **and including**, the size of the pot.

It would be a good idea to read the next paragraph carefully, as staking for pot-limit can be a little confusing at first!

Let us suppose that the blinds in a pot-limit game are £1 and £2. The next player to act after the big blind therefore has to put in £2 to call, but to find out the most they can raise they would need to total up the size of the pot and then add on what it would cost to call. In our example that would be £1 (small blind) + £2 (big blind) + £2 (the cost to call) for a total of £5, as a raise. Therefore, that next player to act would need to put in £7 if they wanted to raise. This would be £2 for the call plus £5 to match the size of the pot once their call had been taken into account.

In other words, the maximum raise is dictated by the size of the pot plus what it would cost to call the last bet. The amount calculated is the amount that the next player could raise by.

However, do note that a raise can never be less than the bet which preceded it unless a player is going all-in. This applies both to fixed- and pot-limit poker. In other words, if a player has bet £5, the next player must either call the wager with £5 or raise to £10 (if they do not wish to fold of course). They would not be allowed to call the £5 and make a raise of, for example, £3 because £3 would not match the size of the last bet made.

No-Limit

No-limit means exactly what it says. Quite simply, in a no-limit game there is no limit to the amount that can be bet! No-limit poker is thought to be the Rolls-Royce of the game because more than any other version it captures the essence of courageous play and outrageous bluffs. This is the version of the game which TV has recently come to love so much.

Having said that there are no limits in a no-limit game, there are a couple of restrictions which newcomers should note. First of all there will be a maximum amount of money which can be brought to the table (table stakes). A game might be entitled '£25 No-Limit' signifying that the maximum amount a player can bring to the table is £25.

This is done because otherwise a player could simply bring an enormous amount of cash into the game and keep staking much more than any of the other players could afford to match. Okay, sometimes they would lose when another player had a good hand and was able to go up against them, but in the medium to long term any player who had an amount of table stakes much bigger than anyone else would stand a considerably greater chance of winning. But note that there is no restriction to what a player can have on the table if they start winning; see the next paragraph for an explanation.

The other restriction in no-limit games is that each player can bet only up to a maximum of their **current** table stakes. So, in a £25 no-limit game a player who has brought £25 to the table can still bet more than £25 on any one hand, providing they have the amount in front of them. Of course, though, if they had brought £25 to the table but had lost a few hands and now only had £15 in front of them this would be the maximum they could bet.

When the two restrictions in a no-limit game are viewed side by side, it becomes clear that any player who, compared to their opponents, is able to build up a sizeable amount of table stakes in one sitting will increase their chances of winning. Remember, though, it will have to be in one sitting because once a player leaves a table they will again be restricted as to what they can re-enter with no matter how much they won originally.

Overall, no-limit poker for anything other than the smallest stakes is probably not the best place for a newcomer to start. It's much better for novices to cut their teeth on fixed-limit and pot-limit tables first.

All-In

No matter what the version of the game, each player will only ever be able to bet up to the amount of cash they have on the table at that time. Therefore situations often occur with fixed-, pot- and no-limit games where a player wants to call a previous bet but does not have enough money to do so.

The rule is that if the player who is short on the required stake wishes to continue they have to go 'all-in'. All-in means that the player puts into the pot the entire amount of stakes they have left in front of them. That player can then no longer continue in the betting for the hand, and a second pot, known as a side pot, will be created for any other bets which the remaining players wish to make on the hand.

The remaining players will then continue to compete for the fresh pot and only those who have contributed will be able to win it. However, once the side pot has been decided there will be a further showdown for the original pot which this time will include the player who had to go all-in. If that player then wins, they take the whole amount of the original pot.

Another thing to note about the all-in rule, which applies mostly to the no-limit version of the game, is that if there are only two players left and one goes all-in, the other only has to match what the first player has bet. For example, player A has £200 in front of them while player B has £300. Player A then goes all-in with their £200, but player B will only have to match the £200 that player A had bet.

The all-in rule is also used in online poker when a player loses their connection to the site. However, online poker sites have very tight restrictions concerning the number of times players can be all-in due to disconnections. Usually they will only allow each player to be 'all-in disconnected' once a day. When a player suffers more than one all-in disconnection during any 24-hour period, they will usually need to contact the poker site operator and have their all-in disconnection limit reset.

This last point is very important to note because, in the early days of online poker, unscrupulous players sometimes used to deliberately disconnect from the site when they didn't want to bet anymore, but still wished to stay in the hand. Hence, the site operators quickly had to come up with a rule to prevent this kind of abuse.

Ring Games / Tournaments

Internet poker can be played either in ring games or in tournaments. Although the mechanics of each game are exactly the same, there is a huge difference between the two in terms of how much money punters need to stake. As you will see, because of this the strong recommendation is that newcomers to online poker start off with tournament play.

Ring Games

Ring games is simply the name given to straightforward games of poker where the players play against each other for real money. It doesn't matter what the version of the game is, or what the staking limits might be; a ring game simply sees the players betting against each other with their own cash.

Tournaments

Tournaments still see players competing against one another, but using a set amount of chips which they will have bought through paying to enter the tournament.

The buy-in for a tournament will be set by the poker site running it. Typically, the buy-in will consist of an amount which goes towards the prize fund, plus a smaller amount which is the fee the sites charge for running the tournaments.

Each player that enters the tournament will receive the same amount of chips, often about £1500 worth, which they will use to play with. Once the start time for the tournament is arrived at, play will begin with players being eliminated when they have no chips left.

The tournament winner will be the last player left with any chips. They will then win the top prize from the prize fund, with the players who were the second and third from last left in winning a smaller share (sometimes those players who were fourth and fifth last in pick up prizes as well, but this depends on the size of the tournament).

Tournaments are offered as 'sit & go', where when the required number of entrants is met the action starts, or as scheduled events where the starting time is advertised in advance and things kick off only at that point. The latter is how the biggest tournaments are run where there are frequently thousands of entrants.

Where a tournament necessitates more than one table being used (multi-table), the site software moves players around the different tables in order to ensure that no entrants just sit on one table biding their time while everyone else is knocked out!

Another feature of online tournaments is that many often give free entry into some of the biggest real-life poker competitions. Many online tournaments are actually free to enter (known as freerolls) and these are an excellent place for newcomers to begin their online poker career at. Generally speaking, tournaments that are not freerolls carry entry fees ranging from as little as £5 upwards.

Also note that many tournaments allow 're-buys'. This simply means that players who are knocked out in the first, say, 60 minutes of the tournament can pay a further fee and buy themselves another set of chips. Although this facility makes tournaments last longer, it does also lead to a bigger prize fund.

As we said above, tournaments are an excellent place for newcomers to start off their online poker career because, providing they have a general idea of how to play the game and how the screens work, they can often compete for long periods for a very small amount of money. They are also great fun because through checking in the lobby screen of the poker site, each player can see how many others remain in the tournament and therefore how close they are to the prize money!

The tactics for tournament play are very different to those required for ring games. To start with, because tournaments are almost always no-limit there is much more 'all-in' play, as players try to knock each other out. Unfortunately, we haven't got the space in this book to look at any tips for playing in tournaments, but the very best way of picking tips up is to simply find the tournaments that are free to enter and get stuck in anyway!

3

Starting Off

I n this chapter we are going to examine what a newcomer to online poker will require to begin playing. But before doing that let's take a walk-through of some of the fears those who have yet to play online often seem to harbour, and thus which stop them enjoying the fun, plus the possible profit, that online poker can bring.

The first thing to say is that anyone considering playing online poker must not think that it is rife with pitfalls and scams. This is simply not the case. If you don't believe this, consider the bricks and mortar environment of Las Vegas. That particular city in the US has long been the casino capital of the world, attracting millions of visitors each year. If all the gambling operations within it were not straight and above board, it simply would not attract so many people. Someone once said, 'You can fool all of the people some of the time, some of the people all of the time, but you cannot fool all of the people all of the time.' That's how it is with Las Vegas, and that's how it is with online poker.

The number of people who now play online poker is so great that if the vast majority of sites were not being run honestly the numbers would soon drop. Because of this the site operators make more money through taking their rake from every pot than they ever could through 'setting up' games. Online poker is now big, big business. Although in the very early days there were a few isolated cases of sites going under (and taking the money of their members with them), many sites today are owned by large corporations. For example, in the UK, Ladbrokes the bookmaker which, in turn, is owned by the Hilton Group, operates a very big site. Even the independent sites, such as PartyPoker, are huge outfits with massive turnovers, so there is little need for them to 'scam' their players.

Please believe it: online poker is perfectly okay to play.

Let's now look at just some of the areas that not only bother those who are thinking of playing but, going by the postings on the numerous online poker forums, also concern those who already play on a regular basis!

The Deal

Online poker sites go to tremendous lengths to ensure security and honest play. As an example, let's consider the way the cards are shuffled before each deal. A look at what one of the top online sites says about this is enlightening:

> No deck of cards in any bricks and mortar cardroom is ever shuffled as well and as thoroughly as we shuffle our cards. Each game, the deck is shuffled 10 times with each shuffle moving each card between one and fifty-one times throughout the deck ... There is no bias to any card, any card patterns or seats at the table.

However, online poker chat rooms still see many players complaining about the computer programs which do the shuffling. A common allegation is that the shuffle is 'bugged' or 'fixed'. In the very early days of online poker there were cases of the algorithms (a set of program instructions) being 'cracked' in order for cheats to be able to know where the cards lay in the deck and thus when they would come out. But this was quickly overcome. Nowadays all the sites are acutely aware of the need to keep their shuffles 'clean'. They fully appreciate that there is more money to be earned through operating an honest and trusted site than the opposite.

Depositing Funds

This is another area that appears to trouble many potential online poker players. They worry about giving their credit card or banking details out over the internet in order to deposit funds. This is an easy one to allay fears about. How many reading this have been victims of a credit card fraud? Of the unfortunate few that have, how many suffered the fraud through using the card online? Chances are that it is very few.

The crucial thing to remember is that the established online poker sites offer the same level of protection, if not higher, against credit- or bank-card fraud that other top online retailers do.

The Hole-Cards

Another worry many inexperienced players have is that their hole-cards can be seen by others, by virtue of someone hacking into the poker site software. But this is another thing not to worry about. There was one well-known instance of hackers managing to do this, but it has been the only one I've ever heard of. No matter what the site, the software sends your hole-cards to your computer alone. So, anyone that wants to see them is going to have to access the software actually running on the server of the online poker operator. That is definitely no easy task!

The River Card

A common complaint on poker chat rooms is how the river card seems to defeat already completed hands more than it does in real-life games. An example might be where a player is already holding, say, three Aces, but is beaten on the river by another player drawing a straight which was only achievable through one specific card coming out.

This does appear to happen slightly more with internet poker than with the real-life version, but is almost certainly due to the fact that the online game is played so much faster. Hence, a greater number of hands are played and therefore all the different occurrences possible with poker will happen more frequently.

The Curse of the Cash-Out

Another complaint often rearing its head on poker chat rooms is called the 'cash-out curse'. This advances the theory that when players cash out (take winnings out of a site) they are marked down to receive a higher-than-normal quota of poor cards the next time they play. Only one answer here. Online poker sites do not care who wins and loses. All they want to see are lots of good pots which they can earn a decent rake from. It is as simple as that. Newcomers should not allow the poker chat rooms to convince them otherwise.

Cheating

Not a week goes by on any online poker forum without at least one or two players complaining they have been cheated at such-and-such a site. The usual argument is that 'I have never experienced as many bad beats as I did last night, and that's in 25 years of playing poker.' Oh dear! It is amazing that players who have taken a thrashing in a £1 / £2 game run by a large site operator like, for example, Ladbrokes, would believe a company of that size could be bothered to cheat an individual player in such a way.

No, players who complain in this fashion are in denial of their own lack of ability. Apart from this, the only other assumption can be that they have failed to appreciate how the faster pace of online poker is going to lead to more hands being played, with this in turn leading to more 'bad beats', more flushes, more straights, and more of everything. So, please do not allow others to convince you that cheating takes place with online poker.

Collusion

Collusion is the biggest fear of online poker players. This form of cheating provokes a lot of debate between poker experts and is a concern for online poker sites. That said, it is not a big problem, but it is the kind of cheating which dishonest players can initiate themselves. This is opposed to most of the other theories regarding cheating, which often accuse the site operators of wrongdoing.

So, what is collusion? The answer is that it can take a number of forms, but they all boil down to the same thing. Colluding is when two players in the same game work together. For example, they might be revealing their hole-cards to one another via the telephone or some kind of internet communication. Alternatively, it could be the same player playing two hands simultaneously at the same table through using two accounts, two phone lines and two PCs.

Either of these collusion methods might well see one of the hands being raised with, and then the other being used for a re-raise. If one hand was very strong, this could be a way of building up a bigger pot through diverting attention from the way it was being played. Aside from this, two hands might be worked together with the purpose of building up the stakes to simply force other players out of the game.

There is no doubt that there is scope for collusion in the ways just described, but in the end neither of the methods would guarantee a pot being won. Indeed, it would probably take a high degree of poker skill for two colluding players – or one player playing two hands – to be able to manipulate even the loosest of games so that a consistent profit was made. Furthermore, would the risk of being caught and suffering their accounts being frozen make it worthwhile, given the limited degree of success collusion would bring? It seems unlikely.

The other thing to remember about collusion is how it can easily take place in real-life games. Indeed, a real-life game is more likely to see two or more players working together because proving what is going on there would be much harder. This is one of the big advantages with online poker. There is an electronic record of every single card dealt, every single hand played, and every single bet made. Consider what one of the top sites said about this not so very long ago:

> We track IP addresses [basically, the identity of every computer
> logged into a game] and match historical playing patterns. This
> enables us to flag if certain players historically play on the same
> table at the same time.

They went on to say:

> We employ monitoring techniques to trap when players have
> repeatedly played unusually. Hand histories are automatically
> reviewed and if, for example, the same player raises and re-raises a
> weak hand more than on just a couple of occasions we will look at
> that player's previous records and investigate if necessary.

Lastly, they made the following point:

> We will quickly investigate if a player starts to fold strong hands
> before the flop. An example might be if a player folds Ace, Queen
> before the flop when another player holds Ace, King.

So, the sites do try to prevent collusion. But there is nothing to stop
any player who has reasonable grounds to suspect collusion in a game
actually notifying the site they are playing on. In almost all cases the
site will investigate. The sophistication of the different sites' software
should never be underestimated, and this enables them to investigate
collusion claims thoroughly.

Poker Robots

This is an interesting topic. Yet another fear among online poker players
is that they might be playing against a robot – or 'bot' for short. A bot
is simply a computer program controlled by either the site or another
player which is designed to play the perfect game of poker. The theory
is that these programs will always win because they are devoid of
emotional thought, operating purely on percentages. But the argument
defeats itself.

Quite simply, a bot might be more efficient at playing the different
card combinations, but because it lacks any form of emotion it cannot
show judgement. Therefore, the extra level of judgement a human being
possesses is always going to give them the edge. The other thing to
remember about bots is that the site operators do not want to see them.
Apart from frightening off players, they also know that if bots ever did
gain the upper hand over humans the sites would simply become a
battleground for different computers each running poker programs.

Having said all that, some sites reportedly already use bots themselves. On certain sites it is said that bots are used to make up the numbers in the play-money games. We will be looking at play-money games shortly, but in this case robots could ensure that even if a player enters into a play-money game where there is nobody else present they could still practise.

The explanations above should allay the fears of people who have been tempted to play online poker but have reservations about actually taking the plunge. But once newcomers decide they are going to start playing, what do they need to begin?

A Computer

This is completely obvious of course, but you cannot play online if you do not have access to a computer. First of all you will require a PC with an operating system of Windows 95 or above. The PC will also need at least 32Mb of RAM and a processing speed of 100MHz or faster, plus 6Mb of free hard drive space. Lastly, your computer screen will require a resolution of at least 800 × 600 pixels with 256 colours. But don't worry, almost all modern PCs meet these requirements and so there is probably no need to rush out and buy a new one!

An Internet Connection

This is another pretty obvious fact, but another thing not to worry unduly about. Today, almost all internet connections will be okay to log through to an online poker site with. However, the strong recommendation is that if you intend to play online poker to any serious degree it is best to have a broadband connection.

The Software to Play

This is very easy to obtain. Nearly every site has a simple set of instructions which, when followed, will enable users to download the poker software. It must be said that a broadband connection makes this a much faster job, but it can be done with just a simple dial-up connection. If, though, anyone encounters problems downloading from any of the sites, they simply need to contact the appropriate site operator's help-desk. If the site operator cannot solve the problem, they will send out a copy of the software on a CD-ROM. Note that obtaining the software is completely free, no matter what method is used.

A Stake

This probably goes without saying, but it needs to be mentioned anyway. Before you start playing poker online, make sure you have the spare money to do so. Always remember that a basic rule of gambling is that you should never bet more than you can afford to lose. Whatever your bankroll (stake), make sure it is money you can afford to be playing with.

Later on in the book we will examine bankroll management in more detail.

So, once an individual has their computer set up, the poker site software downloaded, and their bankroll ready, what do they do next?

Registering

Once you have a site's software installed on your PC, you will need to register with them, which simply translates to filling out an online form with your personal details. Once registered you must then choose an on-screen identity. This can be quite a significant step.

An On-Screen Identity

Setting up an on-screen identity is generally very simple to achieve because all the sites have easy-to-follow instructions for the purpose of guiding newcomers through what they will need to do. But how you wish to be known on the site – in other words your on-screen identity – is solely up to you. We will not spend a great deal of time on this but we do need to make mention of it. Let's see why.

In the early days many online poker players used to spend an inordinate amount of time trying to come up with an on-screen identity which they believed would 'fool' other players. Quite honestly, nowadays this is not worth the effort. Don't waste your time with elaborate names which you think will trick other players into playing poorly (loosely) against you. Although online poker has only been around for a little over nine years, it has still been around long enough for everyone to be wise to this trick.

Just because you take an on-screen identity of, say, 'Granny Muggins', you will probably still not be thought of as a little old lady, playing for some pin money, who can easily be taken out in a head-to-head final round of betting!

On the other hand, some online poker players seem to pick names which they think – note the word 'think' – reflects their personality, or at least the personality they'd like to have. For example, a player who thinks they are incredibly patient and who likes to believe they only play big pots, which they also believe they inevitably win, might go under the name of 'Joe Cool'. But this is also a mistake. If an individual is a good poker player, the last thing they should be doing is using any on-screen identity which might give even the tiniest of hints as to how good they are. As we will see later in the book, knowing how good or bad your opponents are is a crucial part of playing online poker.

Bearing the last point in mind, there is no harm in taking note of what the other players actually play like compared to their on-screen IDs, but don't waste too much time trying to be clever with your own. The strong recommendation is to pick a simple name that you like and which does not shed any light on your ability to play the game.

Also, don't go with a name that gives away what country you are playing in (although on some sites this is unavoidable due to how the on-screen information is picked up from parts of your registration form).

Leave out from your on-screen identity any reference to the country you are playing in because of the following: online poker is played worldwide so you don't want to be advertising that you are playing, for example, at 03.00. To a super-sharp card professional in Las Vegas, where it is still 19.00 the previous day, this is going to suggest that you will be tired and possibly playing because you can't sleep. They might then concentrate on you as the game progresses. Okay, it's unlikely but winning poker players always eliminate even the tiniest of edges which they could be giving their opponents.

Other than this, when it comes to an on-screen ID, don't bother too much about anything else. Instead concentrate upon knowing the cards, knowing the odds and knowing the probabilities, because they are the things that will really help you win money, not your on-screen ID.

However, before leaving the topic of on-screen identities there is one more thing to consider. A lot of poker sites now allow players to select something called an 'avatar' before they start playing. An avatar is simply a computer-generated picture which can be used to represent a player in a game. This is not terribly important so, again, don't spend too much time picking one of these. If anything, newcomers should avoid using an avatar which might give other players a clue as to how good, or poor, they are.

Depositing Money

Once you have set up your on-screen identity, most sites will then prompt you to deposit funds with them in order to be able to play. You can either do so immediately, or skip through to the play-money games. Please, please take full advantage of these play-money games. We will be discussing why they are so important at the start of the next chapter.

However, at some stage you will need to fund your account. The recommendation is to do this only after spending time in the play-money games, simply because then any cash earmarked for deposit can earn interest in your personal account for longer. Obviously, once it moves into your online poker account it will not do so.

Funding your account is fairly simple and there is no need to look at it in any great detail. How accounts are funded is up to the individual, although one of the easiest ways is to open a NETELLER account. NETELLER is a company (owned by eBay) which specialises in moving money between internet sites. It costs nothing to use and is a very quick way of depositing money with an online poker operator. Using NETELLER also overcomes the problem some people have encountered when trying to use their credit card to deposit or withdraw cash. Some credit card companies now block transactions to and from gambling sites. If NETELLER is used, this problem will not be encountered.

A further thing to note about funding is the restrictions. Almost all sites restrict how much an individual can deposit with them during both any 24-hour and 7-day period. They do so to protect themselves against potential fraud, and also to protect their clients against possibly getting in too deep. But you can only find things like this out for yourself through carefully reading the different sites' instructions regarding funding your online poker account.

Lastly, do note that when initially funding an online poker account many sites offer some very good sign-up bonuses. Most of these work through a sum of money being added to the individual's online poker account after they have played a certain number of 'raked' hands.

So, a newcomer would do well to join up with as many sites as possible in order to play enough hands on all of them to pick up the bonuses. Of course, that will be no good if a newcomer then loses more than the bonus amount! However, playing carefully and following some of the ideas that will come later in this book should help prevent this scenario.

Aside from the cash bonuses, the other value in joining up with a lot of sites comes from being able to jump around looking for the loosest games. This is extremely important. As we will examine later on when we discuss ways to win at online poker, one key thing is to find games where your poker skill is greater than that of your opponents. On some of the big US sites this is not always easy, particularly with the higher-stake games. Therefore, it will probably pay to be able to dip into as many sites as you can, interrogating the lobby list to find the real-money games where the percentage of the players going through to the flop is at its highest. Generally speaking, this is an extremely good way of telling where the loose players are.

That's about it with regard to starting off. In the next chapter we will examine those vitally important play-money games.

Practice Makes Perfect

Quite simply, anybody who wants to win at the game needs to know what they are doing. This is pretty obvious, but playing poker, both the real-life and online versions, is all about two things: firstly, knowing the hands and the odds associated with them and, secondly, being better at the game than the other players.

Poker players who win consistently try to find games where there is a high proportion of weaker players. They call these players 'fish'. Fish are players who either don't know how the game works or are simply poor at it. Of course, there are plenty of fish who fall into both categories and these are the ones who are usually gobbled up first. So, newcomers need to equip themselves with at least a reasonable degree of knowledge before they sit down to play for real money. Fortunately, all online poker sites offer more than one way in which this can be achieved. That's what this chapter is all about.

Play-Money Games

Every online poker site offers the facility of play-money / free-money games. Sadly, they are not quite what they seem. There is no free money available! 'Play money' is probably a better name and one which many sites use. Therefore, that's how we will refer to these games in the book.

A play-money game is where the site software allocates a certain amount of chips to each player. The amount of chips will depend upon the level of stakes in whatever play-money game has been selected. Once seated at a play-money table, a player can play exactly as they choose within the rules and limits of the individual game.

Play-money games are the first place that a newcomer to online poker should visit. They are an excellent place to learn how the game works and see the pace it is often played at. They are also the most suitable place to learn about the options each player has on every hand and how they are presented on-screen. We'll take a look at these points in just a moment, but first there is something extremely important to remember about play-money games.

Any newcomer who intends to take their online poker seriously must bear in mind that play-money games are **not** a good place to practise anything other than very basic play. Even then they are not entirely suitable. Because the stakes are not real, players inevitably do not play properly and bet in ridiculous amounts compared to the hands they hold.

Many newcomers to online poker have found that they win considerable sums in play-money games but, once they switch to the real-money version, things become much harder. So, newcomers should use play-money games to become familiar with online poker and for basic practice, but then move on to play in tournaments. As was discussed in chapter 2, tournaments are an inexpensive way to play online for long periods.

The first thing which play-money games are good for is becoming familiar with the **pace** of online poker. The second is as a way of using the different 'click' buttons. The latter is very important. When playing with real cash, newcomers, or anyone else for that matter, do not want to be clicking on the raise button when they meant to fold.

Once a newcomer enters into a play-money game, they should have a good look around. We don't mean look around the room where their computer is either! No, they need to have a look around the table. To start off with, take a look at the on-screen IDs of the other players (to do this on some sites, you'll need to hold the cursor over their seats) and see where they claim to be from. This information is something which players will be asked for when they first register with the site. Don't worry though; the location information displayed at the tables doesn't go down to the level of home addresses.

More importantly, when newcomers look at the other players they should see displayed how much money they have in table-stakes (the amount of money they have in chips). In the play-money games this doesn't really matter, but you'll come to learn that with the real-money tables this information can be of vital importance.

Some sites will even display the internet connection of each of the players. Usually this is defined as excellent, fair or poor. Some show it as slow, okay, good or fast.

Moving on, almost every site will offer the choice over a number of things. These choices will be revealed through clicking on the menu button, or perhaps the dealer's seat, and simply dictate how players wish to interact with the site. They will include such delights as the colour of the table, the colour of the cards, having (or not having) the sound of chips going into the pot, and even a voice asking you if you wish to check, call, fold, etc. Also, you will see something called a 'chat box'.

The lobby screen

A chat box is a small window on the screen where you can interact with the other players through inputting text. Usually the text is in shorthand form, such as 'ty' for 'thank you' or 'nh' for 'nice hand'. An interesting thing to note here is how some players will use these chat boxes to try to influence the game. A common technique is to try to force their opponents into going 'on tilt' (see later in the book) – betting recklessly. If anyone feels that a chat box is likely to start influencing them, the best advice is to turn the option off.

This also applies to any other options available. If anyone believes a particular option is likely to affect their game adversely, they should turn it off. But, on the other hand, newcomers should not be too hasty here. On the play-money games, it is worth experimenting with the different options because some might find that a few of them actually help with concentration, and therefore help them play a better game. Newcomers should use play-money games, to find out how they feel about the different options, and then when they eventually hit a real-money table they will be that little more prepared.

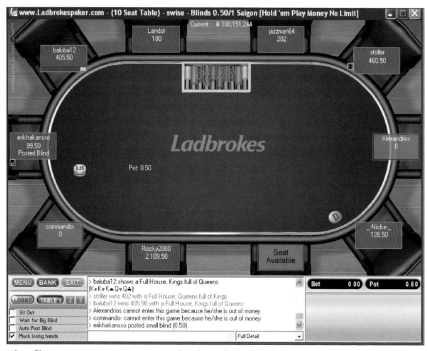

The first screen encountered when logging into a play-money game

Note-Taking

We will cover note-taking in more detail later on in the book, but it needs to be mentioned now because it is a facility which some sites offer that can also be used in the play-money games. An essential part of winning serious money at online poker is to keep notes on your opponents. Okay, there are a lot of people playing poker online, but anyone who intends to play regularly, and **really** wants to win money, will need to make sure that they can identify both the weak and the other equally professional players. Unless an individual is in possession of a supercharged memory, the only way to do this is to take notes.

Notes can be taken by hand, but some sites offer a facility where you can do it online. If that facility does not seem to be available in a menu somewhere, right-click on the seat of another player and see if it comes up then. Of course, if the site being played on does not offer note-taking, it will have to be carried out manually. However it is done though, the bottom line with note-taking is to become familiar with it when playing the play-money games.

Incidentally, the chances are that many of these play-money players will be like you – just starting down the online poker trail. So, keep notes on them in order to try to identify who are fish and who might have a bit of savvy. Keep these notes safe and then when you are ready for the real-money action you can enter into the lobby of your selected sites and seek out the fish (the list of players in each real-money game is always displayed via the lobby). But you can take this a bit further.

Once you have established yourself as a competent real-money player, from time to time why not go back into the play-money games simply to observe them? Look out for any new players who appear to be fish and note down their on-screen identities plus any apparent weaknesses in their play. Then if they ever turn up in the same real-money game as you, you might have an advantage. Indeed, if part of your online poker strategy was built upon periodically scanning for new players with a view to building lists of potential fish, you would probably not go far wrong.

The blind bets have been posted

Obviously, the more substantial your list of fish, the more chance you have of seeing at least some of them in the real-money action. Doing this kind of thing is a small, but nevertheless significant, factor in making money from playing poker online. Okay, a lot of people are now playing online and there is always the possibility that you will never again encounter anyone you have taken notes on. But it costs nothing to do and it might just pay off when you least expect it to.

The hole-cards have been dealt and betting is under way

Action Buttons

Once a game is in progress, the options available to each player when it is their turn will be presented in the form of action buttons. These action buttons give the players the same options regardless of the site being used. But, as is to be expected, the actions available depend upon the situation of the player in a hand.

By returning to chapter 1 and taking a look at some of the terms used in poker, the majority of the available actions will be made clear, but let's run through them quickly now. Depending upon each player's situation, the actions will be:

BET   CALL   RAISE   RE-RAISE   CHECK   FOLD

You will know from chapter 1 what these actions mean, but note there will be slight variations in the options depending upon two things. Firstly, as just mentioned, is the player's situation in the hand. For example, it could be that the **Check** button does not appear because one of the previous players has already made a bet (you will recall that the check option is only available until a bet is made in a betting round). Or, it could be that a player is the first one to have the option to make a bet. In this case the **Call** button will be missing.

The second reason the buttons may look slightly different is because the amount of money required to execute the selected option will also appear. Hence, the **Call** button might have a 5 next to it **(Call 5)** in order to show that 5 chips is the amount required to match the last bet.

Overall, there is little to be gained in running through what these action buttons look like on the screen. Having a basic knowledge of what they mean and then expanding upon that knowledge in play-money games is the best way to go. However, what we must do is examine the topic of **pre-action** buttons because they can lead newcomers into serious trouble!

Pre-Action Buttons

These are unique to online poker and a very important part of the game. All online poker sites feature them and they cannot be ignored. Pre-action buttons give players the opportunity to select their actions in **advance** of when the play actually reaches them. Designed to speed up the game, they can be real traps for the unwary. So, the play-money games must be used to become familiar with them.

The pre-action buttons give players exactly the same choices as the option buttons themselves, but in some cases also allow a player to do one thing or another on the same button. For example, one pre-action button is **Check / Fold**. Using this pre-action button allows a player to check if nobody bets before them, but fold if they do. Incidentally, the clever thing about this is how the poker sites have their software set up so that the buttons change as different options either become available or disappear.

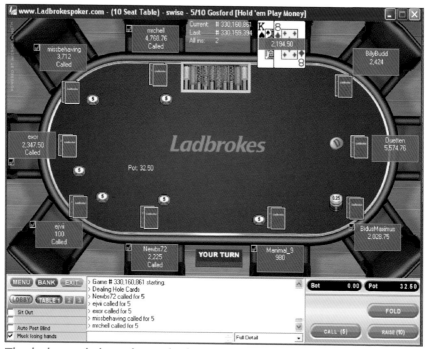

The hole-cards have been dealt

Playing in a play-money game is definitely the best way to become familiar with this facility. But please note that if you use pre-action buttons at the wrong time you can give experienced players clues as to the strength of your hand. Giving away clues about your hand is known as an 'online tell'. We'll examine online tells later in the book but here is a good example to be going on with.

Imagine a player was in a game with seven others. The stakes were £5 / £10 and the player was the first to act. The initial deal was good to the player and they were left sitting with the following as their hole-cards:

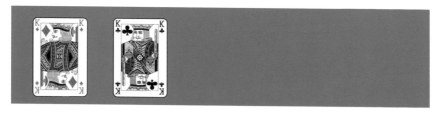

In the first round of betting, the player managed to raise the stakes and still keep another four players in with them. The flop (the first set of three community cards) was dealt and they came up as:

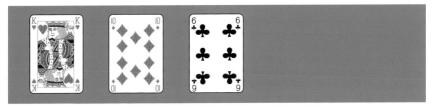

So, the player now had at least three Kings, a very strong hand. At that point they would have been presented with a choice of pre-action buttons. These were likely to have been:

(The exact choice of buttons will have depended upon the game, the site, the stakes, etc.)

The player's position in the hand was now pretty strong. Okay, there were four other players still in the game, which will have sounded a note of caution, but the player clearly had a great chance of taking the pot. So, the last thing they would have wanted to do was give away a clue about their hand.

However, that is exactly what they could have done through jumping in and hitting any of the pre-action raise buttons **as soon as they were presented**. Had they selected the **Raise Any** button, any of the other players who were on the ball would immediately have realised how the player was prepared to raise any bet regardless of what it was. **This is because through using the pre-action Raise Any button they will have told the poker software what they wanted to do before their turn actually came around.** Although their wish will not have been executed until their turn arrived, that wish will have then been executed with lightning speed. This is the kind of thing good players notice and take as a clue.

Nowadays, in a £5 / £10 game the standard of play is such it is likely that at least two of the remaining players, possibly more, would have been frightened off and therefore folded. **Rashly using the pre-action button midway through a hand is one of the big online tells with internet poker.** To avoid giving yourself away in the manner just described, the recommendation is to show some caution when using the pre-action buttons **during** a hand.

Tick-Boxes

As well as the pre-action buttons, online players can also make decisions in advance about certain aspects of the game through using the tick-boxes, which all the sites incorporate into their game pages.

The most obvious example of these is when players are offered the chance to 'auto-post' their blind. This one simply allows a player to have their small and large blind bets posted automatically whenever it is their turn to make them. Any player who does not have this box ticked will be prompted each time they need to put in their blind bets. No big deal there of course, but it is surprising how quickly the blind bets come around. It also allows anyone who might have to be away from their computer momentarily to make their blind bets in an automatic fashion. If this button is used, they will not delay the hand and also not run the risk of being 'timed out' if they fail to make their blind bet before the allotted response period has elapsed.

The flop cards have been dealt

A further pre-action tick-box is 'sit-out'. This can be used when a player wants to be away from their screen for a short time, but does not wish to leave the game entirely. By ticking the 'sit out' box, they will then be left out of the subsequent deals until indicating otherwise.

However, the most important pre-action tick-box is the one which automatically allows a player to fold a losing hand at the showdown without the other players seeing it. Here the tick-box will generally be labelled as 'Muck Lost' or 'Muck Losing Hands' – muck being another term in poker for fold. The strong recommendation here is that all players put a tick in this box. If they don't, they will always have their beaten showdown cards revealed to the other players.

If a player goes through to a showdown, but is then beaten, it is generally poor strategy to allow the other players to see their cards. Earlier in the hand it might be slightly less important, but it is still a good idea to always select 'muck cards' anyway. Otherwise, at the showdown, a player's whole hand will be revealed and their opponents

The player called 'Mr Chell' is deciding whether to bet after the flop

The turn cards have been dealt

will be able to see precisely what they were doing. Some would argue that players who occasionally wish to 'advertise' they were bluffing might want to reveal their cards, but that can still be done through unticking the 'muck cards' box close to the end of the hand (but then remembering to re-tick it). So, best advice is to always tick the 'muck cards' box, and then you will not accidentally reveal your losing cards to the other players.

With that ends our look at the ways newcomers can become familiar with online poker through the play-money games. The critical thing for newcomers is to use the play-money games to be ready for the real-money action. Once in a real-money game, a newcomer does not want to be left sitting there puzzled as to what they are seeing in front of them, however minor that may be.

Once familiar with play-money games, the next place for newcomers to go is tournaments, where they often can play for long

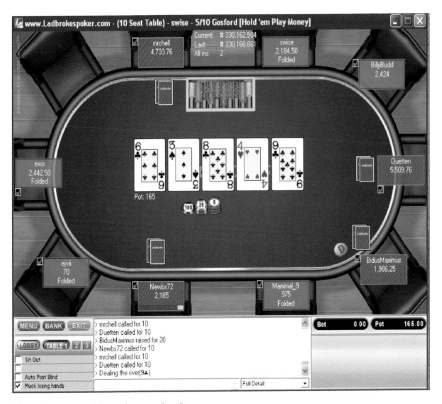

The river card has been dealt

periods at little cost. But we haven't got the space in this book to examine tournament strategy. Anyway, because the cost of entering them is so low (even free in many cases), players can simply teach themselves. No, next stop is a look at some basic winning techniques for the real-money games.

The showdown, with player called 'Mr Chell' winning the hand,
beating player called 'Exor' in the process

5

Winning Techniques – Basic Strategy to the Flop (Ring Games)

Okay, now we have arrived at the point where a newcomer to online poker is ready to start playing for real money. Because there are more of them than tournaments, the techniques we will examine in the next few chapters are concerned with ring games. Strategy for tournament play is not that different, except for the fact that more aggression is needed. But that will become clear as newcomers take part in tournaments. In the end, though, ring games are where the money can be won on a much more regular basis. They are an internet poker player's bread and butter.

Newcomers must first be aware that there is more to winning at online poker than just having knowledge of the cards and the way to play them. As was mentioned in preceding chapters, the very first thing that winning players do is look for the games where there are 'fish' (incidentally, the better online poker players are known as 'sharks'). This begins with finding the correct site, game and table.

For the purposes of what follows we are discussing fixed-limit games because they are the ones which newcomers should kick off in.

Selecting a Site, a Game and a Table

This is where winning players start making their profits. Careful selection of a site, and even more so of a game and a table, is the first step in playing online poker to win.

However, it is worth remembering that almost everyone starts off as a fish with internet poker! Those that graduate through learning to play properly become the winners (the sharks) and those that don't remain losers (fish). In real-life poker the best players try to find weak opponents sitting at weak tables, but the mechanics of actually getting to play on such tables are not that easy to master because of the way casino poker tables are set up. However, there is no such problem with internet poker.

Selecting a Site

Selecting an online poker site is fairly simple. Nowadays there are a tremendous number to choose from. But first and foremost make sure that the site you intend to play on is a reputable one. It would be extremely disappointing to win money at online poker and then not be able to get to it because the site has gone bust or committed some form of fraud. Don't worry though, the vast majority of sites are fine, with some very large companies (like Ladbrokes in the UK) operating them.

The other thing to consider when selecting a site is that the bigger and better known it is, the more players will be on it. Yes, that's fairly obvious, but more players mean the greater the chance of fish swimming around! This, cruel though it might seem, is a major consideration when selecting a site.

Something to note here is that a site owned by, say, Ladbrokes or William Hill, might attract more fish than PartyPoker or Paradise Poker. This is due to the fact that these sites will appeal to 'cross-over' punters, ie those who have perhaps come to learn of the online poker world through the betting shop. Bear this in mind.

Another thing to note when considering who might be playing on a site is that some tend to attract more players from certain areas of the world than others do. Without wishing to upset anyone, in my observations the inherent characteristics of some nationalities seem to make them less suitable for playing poker than others. As an example, Scandinavian people appear to make better players than those from countries where the blood runs a little hotter! Therefore, newcomers, providing they believe they will be able to play in a controlled fashion, may first do better on sites where there is an abundance of hot-headed individuals.

Bonuses / Rakes

As we mentioned in the previous chapter, another consideration when selecting a site is the bonuses they offer. Most sites will offer bonus chips for players making their first ever deposits. Hence, providing they have a decent-enough-sized bankroll, a newcomer should consider signing up with as many sites as they can. In that way they will be able to take advantage of all the bonuses on offer. But do remember that most sites only add the bonuses after a certain number of raked hands have been played. Following this, a lot of sites offer bonuses for regular play, but only after a qualifying number of hands each month. Regular players should be aware of these bonuses because it would be foolish to miss out on getting something for nothing.

Of course, it would be equally foolish to select a site on the back of the bonuses being offered, only then to find they take a bigger rake than most of their rivals. Therefore, check this kind of thing out as well.

Always prefer sites which have a lot of games running, or at least a reasonable number for the times you think you will be playing. This is because more games signify more tables, and that means more fish. One of the biggest sites in the world is PartyPoker. This site is busy most of the time. But note that many of their online players are not based in this country. Hence, the peak times at PartyPoker, as at a lot of sites, are when the UK is sleeping. That's okay if a UK-based player doesn't mind a bit of night work, but it is worth looking at the Ladbrokes site if you want to see peak traffic a little earlier on. Ladbrokes has its highest level of activity between 20.00 and 23.00.

Another interesting point about the Ladbrokes site is that it does not allow US-based players to play on it. For a newcomer this is very important. On the whole there is no doubt that US players are slightly better than those from the rest of the world. In the US lots of people play poker at home from an early age. Many continue to play the game at college, with the result that US players are generally harder to beat online. So, Ladbrokes is a good site to play on, as no players from across the pond are allowed there.

Selecting a Game

You will only be able to select a game once you are in the lobby of your chosen site (or sites, because there is nothing to stop you playing in multiple places, although this isn't a recommendation for beginners).

The most obvious thing to look for when selecting a game is the level of stakes required for it. No matter how experienced a player is, they should never play in a game where the stakes run higher than they are happy with. This includes playing in a game with higher stakes just because it appears there are plenty of fish about. Despite the opposition being easier, any players who take part in games with higher stakes than they are comfortable with run a risk. Plenty of newcomers to online poker have found to their cost that, due to a run of poor hands, the sight of their chips quickly disappearing soon begins to ruin their concentration. The result is that the fish get off the hook.

The other main consideration when selecting a game is a fairly obvious one. Quite simply, anyone who wants to win money from playing online poker should always go for the game they are best at. This book is very much concerned with Texas Hold 'em, but if a newcomer starts to find they are better at Seven-card Stud or Omaha, these are the games they should head for. In the end, a player will usually enjoy more success if they first go for the game they are best at and then try to beat any fish that might be playing in them.

Selecting a Table

At almost all sites, Texas Hold 'em will easily be the most popular game. As you might expect, because of this there will normally be a large number of tables playing it. The first job will be to select the table that offers the best chance of winning. Providing it doesn't involve chancing your arm by going into a game where the stakes are higher than you are comfortable with, you should select your table from the following criteria.

The table that has the highest percentage of players going through to the flop is probably the loosest. This is pure common sense. Supposing that in the lobby of your chosen site you find that Texas Hold 'em is being played on six tables. In the lobbies all sites should display the following information about their tables:

- The number of players currently at the table (with possibly their names as well) plus the number of players waiting to join that game
- The average number of players seeing out each flop
- The average pot size
- The number of hands dealt per hour.

Talk about being given great information to start with! Let us imagine that you wish to play a game where the stakes are £1 / £2. On most sites the information for games of that level will look something like this:

Table name	Stakes	Average players per flop	Average amount per pot	Hands per hour	Number of players
Nijinsky	£1 / £2	61%	£31	71	9
Shergar	£1 / £2	37%	£26	74	9
Motivator	£1 / £2	19%	£30	90	9
Mill Reef	£1 / £2	23%	£19	81	9
Troy	£1 / £2	21%	£21	80	9
Sea Bird II	£1 / £2	42%	£33	54	9

So, what does this tell us? Simple: table Nijinsky has the highest number of players lasting through to the flops. Therefore, this is almost certainly playing as the loosest table. The average pot size is decent – something else suggesting that more players are staying in longer. This is further borne out by the lower number of hands per hour. Obviously, the longer the players stay in the action, the fewer hands which can be played.

On the other hand, a table to avoid is Motivator. With a low number of players going through to the flop, this appears to be a tough table with few fish swimming around.

Of course, this information should not be treated as the be-all and end-all. To start with, you will not know whether the statistics for each table have been gleaned from the last hour, the last 24 hours, or since the table first appeared on the poker site. But it is still information worth having because you can bet your life that in their haste for some action the vast majority of online poker players take absolutely no notice of things like this.

Choosing a Seat

Once you decide upon a table, choosing your seat is something else worth mentioning. If a table looks okay in terms of the game and the players, and if you do get the chance to choose your seat, try to remember the following.

Unless you are really impatient to get stuck in, always choose the seat furthest away from the blinds. When first sitting down at a table you will be given the option of posting a blind immediately, or waiting for your turn to come around to do so. If you choose the latter, you will not be dealt into any hands until you have posted the big blind. Bearing this in mind, the recommendation is that you try to pick a seat some distance from the blinds. Then, do not choose to put in a blind straight away. Instead, sit tight and watch the pattern of the game. This will be of assistance in trying to see how the other players are performing.

Perhaps there might be a couple of fish out there, unwittingly giving themselves away through loose play. Or perhaps someone will be 'on tilt' (playing poorly because they have hit a losing streak). Naturally, there might not be any of this going on, but the professional approach is to sit tight, watching for a few hands. Then when it is your turn to post the big blind you'll possibly be able to play your first hand with knowledge that you would not possess if you had dived straight in. And what will have been the cost of waiting? That's right, nothing except a bit of time and patience.

Money on the Table

So, you have now selected your site, your game and your table. At this point you will be off and running. However, even in the right game with weak players, a good player still has to practise the correct strategy to win money. This can actually start with how much cash a player takes to the table in chips.

The first thing a player needs to do once sitting down at a game is buy in. This means to put on the table the amount of chips you want to play with. The feeling among seasoned poker players is that you should always enter a game with the biggest pile of chips you are allowed.

With real-life games, players often like to appear a high-roller from the start. Their feeling is that this might put them at a psychological advantage over their opponents. But in many ways this thinking is flawed. Real-life games tend to see the players stay in for long periods. Hence, if a game has been running for five hours, a player with a big pile of chips may not have actually won them; they may still be sitting on them from when they first bought in. But observant opponents will always remember when a player bought in big and so once that player has taken part in a few hands any perceived advantage they thought their buy-in gave them may well have been lost. In real-life games it is more about how a player actually plays their cards rather than the pile of chips they buy in with.

However, with internet poker things are different. Online games see players come and go with great frequency. Hence, if a player enters a game and sees that another player has a large pile of chips they will have no idea whether that player has been winning, losing, or has simply stayed even.

As an example, if a player enters a £3 / £6 game where the typical buy-in is £200 (remember, you can first observe a game without playing), it can be an advantage to bring £400 to the table. Anyone who comes into the game after that player, providing the player in question has not quickly lost a large chunk of their chips, will tend to think they have managed to double their buy-in rather than having entered the game with it in the first place. It is surprising how naive many online poker players can be. This can often lead to players giving more respect than is necessary to someone with a big pile of chips. The result is that the player with the bigger pile of chips can occasionally pull off bluffs with relatively poor cards.

However, let's sound a note of caution here. Just because you buy in big does not mean that you need to play big all the time. As we will see in a moment, 'selective / aggressive' play is the key.

Of course, there is another very practical reason for buying in big. Once you are at a table, many sites place restrictions on how much you can re-buy in with if you are unfortunate enough to lose all of your chips. Therefore, it is better to make sure you have enough in front of you to play for the length of time you have set aside, rather than possibly be disappointed later on.

Selective / Aggressive

The best way for any player to approach online poker, and this is even more true if they are a newcomer, is to adopt a policy of playing selectively and aggressively. For short this is called selective / aggressive. Putting it simply, this means being selective about the hands that are played, but when a hand is played it should be played aggressively. However, the selection of which hands to play is very much dependent upon a player's position in the betting. Position is an absolutely crucial part of Texas Hold 'em.

The nearer a player is to the dealer's right, the later they will have to act. Thus, they will have more chance to see what their opponents are doing. This makes a difference to how different sets of hole-cards should be played – shortly we'll examine some charts that will help with this.

This is probably an appropriate time to mention that it is impossible to be really precise about Texas Hold 'em. This is a game full of nuances with many different things needing to be taken into account. For example, an internet game of ten players would need to be played differently from one where there are only five. (Games where there are fewer than six players are generally known as 'short-handed'.)

Incidentally, playing poker online is still a little like the Wild West! On some sites a game of ten people can be a real shoot-out with bets flying in from every angle. In these cases it is much harder to play even what is a strong hand, as there is always the fear that someone will have a better one. Even if a player judges they have a reasonable hand, the amount of betting which takes place can test their resolve, especially with hole-cards which fall into the category of being 'close to really strong'.

Anyway, here is an example of selective / aggressive play. With Texas Hold 'em the best hole-cards to have are a pair of Aces. With a pair of bullets (just one of their many nicknames), a player has a good chance of winning the pot regardless of their betting position in that particular hand. But there are still five community cards to be dealt and so plenty can happen before the showdown.

Therefore, a player with a pair of Aces as their hole-cards needs to make a move early on in order to try to force at least some of their opponents to fold. Obviously, the higher the number of players that stay in the deal, the greater the chance that one of them will achieve a hand which eventually beats the player holding the pair of Aces. So, the player holding the Aces should be looking to make a strong bet as early as they can in order to reduce the chances of being beaten later on.

However, if only poker was as simple as that! As the idea is to make money, the player holding the Aces would not want all of their opponents to fold, otherwise they would win nothing but the blind bets – and one of them might be theirs to start with. Thus, the basic strategy in this situation is to make a big enough bet to kill off some of the other players, but small enough to keep the players with the second, and possibly third, best hands in the deal. Of course, there is still no guarantee that making a big bet on a pair of hole-card Aces will lead to the pot being scooped, but it might help. (Incidentally, when a player who is holding a pair of Aces as their hole-cards does not win the pot, the saying is that the 'Aces have been cracked'.)

Selective / aggressive play is all about playing the **right** hands in an aggressive enough fashion to win the pots. But remember that the level of aggression does depend on the hand, and also on a player's position at the table.

Because position is so important in Texas Hold 'em, experts in the game have devised a general strategy for how players should play their hole-cards depending upon where they sit in relation to the dealer's disc. As we have just seen, after that it is more down to the player to decide what to do, but for newcomers in particular the tables which follow shortly are a good starting point in learning what hands they should select to play, and then how aggressively. However, before we look at them, consider the following because it really does hammer home why playing the 'right' hole-cards is so important.

With Texas Hold 'em, for the cost of one betting interval, all the players see 71% of the cards that can make up their hands. Think about that for a moment. All the players receive two face-down cards and then come five community cards. The flop produces the first three, the turn the fourth, and the river the last. Each player can use five of the seven cards in any combination they like to produce their best poker hand.

The flop takes place after the first betting interval has finished and so at that point five of the seven cards will be in play. That's 71% of the total for the cost of just one set of betting. This is one of the reasons the game is so popular, and also why the betting before the flop is so critical.

What follows now are three tables which give an indication of what hole-cards should be played from what position. The assumption for these tables is that it is a ten-player game. Positions 1 and 2 have to make the blind bets, so the tables show positions 3 through to 10 (the dealer's position).

However, do remember that while these tables are a good general guide they should not be taken as gospel. Also, there are some important notes to accompany them:

- Early positions are positions 3 and 4.
- Middle positions are 5, 6 and 7.
- Late positions are 8, 9 and 10.
- In the middle positions, the Suited and Non-suited hands should really only be played if the pot has not previously been raised.
- In the late positions, the majority of the hands making their first appearance in the tables should again only be played if the pot has not been raised first. For newcomers it would also be a good idea to only play these hands if at least 70% of the other players have already folded.

Playable hands from positions 3 and 4

Hole-cards ▼	Combination ▼
Pairs	Aces through to 7s inclusive
Suited	Ace with King, Queen, Jack, 10
	King with Queen, Jack, 10
	Queen with Jack, 10
	Jack with 10, 9
	10 with 9
Non-suited	Ace with King, Queen, Jack, 10
	King with Queen, Jack
	Queen with Jack, 10

Playable hands from positions 5, 6 and 7

Hole-cards	Combination
▼	▼
Pairs	**As table, but add:**
	5s and 6s
Suited	**As table, but add:**
	Ace with 9, 8, 7, 6
	King with 9
	Queen with 9, 8
	Jack with 8
	10 with 8
	9 with 8
Non-suited	**As table, but add:**
	King with 10
	Queen with Jack, 10
	Jack with 10

Playable hands from positions 8, 9 and 10

Hole-cards	Combination
▼	▼
Pairs	All Pairs
Suited	**As tables, but add:**
	Ace with 5, 4, 3, 2
	King with 8, 7, 6, 5, 4, 3, 2
	Queen – no change from previous table
	Jack with 7
	10 with 7
	9 with 7, 6
	8 with 7, 6
	7 with 6, 5
	6 with 5
	5 with 4
Non-suited	**As tables, but add:**
	King with 9
	Queen with 9
	Jack with 9, 8
	10 with 9, 8
	9 with 8, 7
	8 with 7

These tables are a good starting point for newcomers, but what they may also find interesting is the next table, which indicates the chances of being dealt the major combinations of hole-cards.

Hole-cards	Odds
Defined Pocket Pair (two cards the same)	220/1
Ace-King suited	331/1
Ace-King non-suited	110/1
Ace with less than Jack but suited	36/1
Ace with less than Jack, non-suited	11/1
Any Pair	16/1
Any two cards same suit	3.25/1
Any two cards, connected and suited	47/1
Any two cards connected, non-suited	15/1

Finally, here are two more tables concerned with hole-cards. The first shows the probability of another player **not** holding an Ace (or any other card for that matter) if you **do have** one.

Number of players	Probability
2	88.2%
3	77.5%
4	67.5%
5	58.6%
6	50.5%
7	43%
8	36.4%
9	30.5%
10	25.3%

This second table illustrates the probability of no other player holding an Ace (or any other card) if you **also do not** have one.

Number of players	Probability
2	84.5%
3	70.9%
4	59%
5	48.6%
6	39.7%
7	32.1%
8	25.6%
9	20.1%
10	15.6%

Hole-Cards

As we have seen, with Texas Hold 'em a selective / aggressive strategy needs to be based on the two face-down cards (the hole-cards), plus a player's position at the table relative to the dealer. A major fault with many online poker players is how they simply refuse to fold hole-cards which they cannot win with in the long run. Sure, if they want to play a bluff they should stay in with weak hole-cards, especially if they are one of the last to act, but even then if they do it too frequently they will soon be replenishing their online poker accounts.

A pair will be dealt to a player as their hole-cards on average every 17 hands. The difference in value between the types of pairs widens rapidly between Kings and Queens and below. Jacks, 10s and 9s should be regarded as medium pairs with the rest as low.

After a pair the next best thing to have with your hole-cards is an Ace and a high 'kicker'. The kicker is the name given to the lower of the two hole-cards. So, an Ace with a King is better than an Ace with a Queen, and so on. Indeed, an Ace with a high kicker, especially if they are of the same suit ('suited'), can often be more valuable than a medium or low pair. There is an obvious reason for this. If a player holds an Ace and a King, and then an Ace appears on the flop, they will have the highest pair:

Player holds   **The flop produces**

The player therefore holds a pair of Aces with a King as the kicker. Straight away they know they have the best pair. Okay, it can be equalled by someone who holds the same value cards, but they will still have something very substantial to continue betting with, especially in a short-handed game. This is due to the fact that only two pairs or better can actually beat them. Let's look at another example.

Player holds   **The flop produces**

In this instance the player will have at least the equal second highest pair (Kings) with an Ace as the kicker – another nice set of cards to continue with, again especially in a short-handed game.

Next up in value is an Ace with a small kicker. If these are non-suited, it is generally not that good a hand. It certainly does not offer the potential which a combination that could become a flush or a straight does. But again, think twice if you are not facing many opponents. In these cases the Ace becomes more valuable.

After an Ace with a small kicker are unpaired high cards. If the hole-cards are King and Queen, or even as low as King and 10, they might be okay before the flop, but will be vulnerable afterwards, especially if they are non-suited. As a rule of thumb, if you have a card below a 9 with a non-suited King you may well struggle after the flop, even in a short-handed game.

Flushes and straights often win poker hands, but to have the best chance of obtaining them a player's hole-cards need to be suited, or consecutive, or both. Generally speaking, combinations of suited cards in value from 9, 8 down to 5, 4 come out at about the same rank as a small pair. The advice is that suited hole-cards (and even more so non-suited) below a Jack which cannot be part of a straight, such as 9, 4 or 10, 3 should generally be folded, even in short-handed games.

Combinations of cards which are below the value of those we have already discussed should generally be folded, no matter how many players are in the game.

Remember, far too many online poker players continue with hands that they are not going to win with in the long run. Be selective – as in selective / aggressive.

The Flop

It is a golden rule of Texas Hold 'em that no matter how good a player's first two cards are, the flop is what makes them stand up. **The flop must fit a player's hand.** If a hand fails to improve as a result of the flop, a player should normally fold. The only exception is when someone picks up a draw to a very strong hand. (A 'drawing hand' means when the flop gives a chance to improve a hand to something considerably stronger through 'drawing' the required cards on the turn or the river. It is also the term used when the hole-cards give the chance of doing the same thing from the flop.) An example follows – assume the player is in a late betting position:

Player holds   **The flop produces**

Although their hole-cards looked moderate, the player continued in the betting because the cards were suited and because of the player's late position in the betting. However, the flop has now given the player a chance to 'draw' a straight flush if the turn and the river happen to bring the following two cards (admittedly a long shot):

Alternatively, a Jack of any suit will give the player a straight. Given that they are sitting in a late betting position, they are now in better shape, although it is still a long shot they will be dealt the cards they require.

An excellent rule of thumb is not to continue beyond the flop without at least a strong pair accompanied by a high kicker. Two pairs would be considerably better, and trips (three of a kind) better still. The latter would put you in with a very good chance of winning the pot, especially if the game is short-handed.

Aside from the hands we have just looked at, if a player has a straight or flush draw they should only really continue if they have at least two opponents left in the pot. In other words, the size of the pot should be big enough to balance out the risk of their desired hand not coming off.

Again though, poker is rarely as straightforward as the examples we have been considering. Often the flop will be of enough assistance for a player to think about continuing, but not enough for them to be sure. Let's look at an example of that.

Supposing after the flop a player has been left with a medium pair and the outside chance of a straight if the correct cards come through on the turn and the river. In this situation the cards might be as follows:

Player holds   **The flop produces**

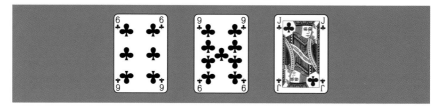

This player is now in possession of a pair of 8s, and there is the possibility of a straight flush if the following cards are dealt:

There is also the possibility of a straight, three of a kind, plus more (work them out for yourself).

It looks quite tempting, but if another player is still in the betting there is the distinct possibility they will have a higher pair than 8s. So, if the player stays in for the turn they'll probably need to achieve **at least** trips to win. Furthermore, if on the turn they don't see an 8 of any suit (or a 6, 9 or Jack) they will be betting on an 8 coming out on the river. If it doesn't, they will hold a pair of 8s, and that will be a weak hand to have bet into the last card with. (This scenario doesn't take into account how the board 'hand' might itself improve simply because the board hand is available to everyone.)

A critical thing to remember about the flop is that all the cards in it belong to all of the players. This might sound obvious but it is no good becoming overexcited if a pair of Aces appear on the flop, because that means everyone now holds at least that hand. That said, if a player already has either one or two Aces in the hole things will be different!

Of course, one of the appeals of Texas Hold 'em is that the flop might help your hand, either making it stronger or suddenly giving you a good set of cards from what may have looked a moderate position. (Perhaps, though, the latter is something that will appeal more to a gambler than a selective / aggressive player.)

A good example is where a player might be betting from a late position on a pair of 9s. Depending upon how many players are left in, this will either look a good, or at least a reasonable, hand. Let's suppose it is only looking reasonable. If the flop produced another 9, the player will have suddenly moved into a position of considerable strength with a good three of a kind.

But with poker there is always a note of caution to be sounded. Hence, if a player holds a low to middling pair as their hole-cards and a third one of similar rank appears on the flop to give three of a kind, the player still needs to be careful about betting too aggressively. Again, it will largely depend upon their position in the betting, but newcomers should always remember that a higher triple could be out there. Here is a good example.

Player holds   **The flop produces**

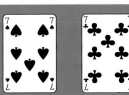

The player now holds three 7s, but the Ace and the Queen in the flop could spell trouble. It is only going to take someone to be already holding a pair of Aces or Queens as their hole-cards and the player will be way behind.

Naturally, there are many more combinations than those we have looked at which could change either your own or your opponents' hands, but the point is that newcomers must not be carried away by what at first seems like a good set of cards. The motto is 'Do not fall in love with your hand until you are pretty sure it is the best one on the table'.

Online poker players should always think carefully first, but then if they do decide to play a hand the recommendation is that they go in hard enough to blow away anyone who might be bluffing, or perhaps simply chancing their arm with a low hand. **Again, selective / aggressive play is the key.** Let's look at one more example.

Player holds	**The flop produces**

The player now holds two pairs, seemingly a reasonable hand. Well it is certainly not to be sneezed at, but it is crucial to remember that everyone now holds at least a pair of 7s as well. Another player has only got to be holding an Ace and the player with the 4s and 7s will be well behind. The only way they could now win is if the turn or the river brought the cards that would give them a full house or better. But then the same thing could happen to the player holding the Aces and 7s! Following are some golden rules to remember about the flop.

- The flop defines each player's hand. If the flop doesn't fit into their hole-cards, a player should usually fold, unless they are in a very late betting position and many of their opponents have folded before them.

- When the flop gives a player a strong hand, it must be remembered that they still need to give some of their opponents a chance to stay in the pot. If they go in too strong too early, they will frighten most of the other players away and thus the pot will probably be a small one. So, while selective / aggressive play is still the key, over-aggressiveness will kill pots off without much being in them.

- However, bearing the above point in mind, players must still play aggressively enough to stop any of the other players drawing a card on the turn or the river that then beats them. In other words, unless you have an absolutely top-notch hand you should try to eliminate at least some of your opponents with the first set of bets.

- The best hands to be aggressive with are those that hold multiple possibilities, such as a high pair with a strong kicker.

- If a player is in a late betting position and nobody has called the blinds before the flop, they should at least consider raising on any pair, an Ace with a good kicker, or a King with a Queen, Jack or 10 – especially in short-handed games. In these situations the two blind hands may well then fold and the player will have 'pinched' a pot. But even if one or both of the blinds continue, the player still has the flop, the turn and the river to help them.

A Final Note

One thing you may have noticed with this chapter is that in some places it tends to give slightly contradictory advice. Well, welcome to playing internet poker! There are no hard-and-fast rules which can be laid down as the perfect strategy – in the end, players often need to use their own judgement. But remember that a selective / aggressive approach will definitely keep newcomers in games longer than a reckless one will.

6

Winning Techniques – Basic Strategy from the Flop Onwards (Ring Games)

So far we have looked at ways to consider playing up to the flop. Let's stop for a moment and consider where we are. A player has received a reasonable, or perhaps even a good, set of hole-cards and has stayed in the betting with at least a call. The flop has come along and done one of three things:

1 Fitted the player's hole-cards to give them a really good hand.
2 Done absolutely nothing for their hole-cards and therefore forced them into folding.
3 Improved their hand a little, but probably not enough to get their heart beating that bit quicker. However, the possibility still remains that the turn and the river could give them something special.

What is done after the flop is also crucially important. In fact, some poker experts argue that the betting on the flop is the most important of all. This is because the chances of improving a hand on the turn and the river can be compared against what it will cost to stay in the pot. Hence, we will consider something called 'pot odds'.

Pot odds

It is easy to know what to do in the first two situations, listed above, but the third is the most common for players to encounter and so it is here that good poker players make use of their knowledge of pot odds.

The idea is to compare the odds of completing what a player believes will be a winning hand against the current payout for doing so. In other words, a player looks at the odds they will be paid out at against the odds of actually pulling off a hand which they think will win. If it is 8/1 against them pulling off the hand, but the payoff is 9/1, they would generally go ahead and stay in the deal. Calculating these odds is quite easy, but to make it crystal clear let's break it down into some easy-to-follow steps.

1   Determine the value of the chips already in the pot, to include those being put in during the current betting round.
2   Try to estimate what the other players might bet into the pot after you have acted. This is the tricky bit, but if you have been watching your opponents closely you should at least have an idea of whether they are playing carefully, carelessly or selective / aggressively. From that you should be able to make a reasonable estimate about the amount they will then bet.
3   Divide the estimated amount of the pot by what is needed to call the last bet. For example:

The pot is currently £20. You estimate that it will grow to £25 before the betting round ends, providing nobody else raises after you have acted. (This is a good example of where being last to act is such an advantage.) You have to put £5 into the pot to call. Hence, divide £25 by £5 to arrive at pot odds of 5/1. (With your £5 the pot becomes £30. So, 30 divided by 5 is 6, which translates to odds of 5/1.)

However, if you were not the last to act and another player raised after you had had your turn, a recalculation would then have been necessary.

4   Compare the pot odds against the odds of drawing to a hand which you believe will win (remember, drawing simply means obtaining a better set of cards). Should the odds against obtaining that hand be less than the calculated pot odds, you should continue betting.

What follows shortly is a table which will show the odds against drawing to a better hand from the flop through to the turn and the river. This table is based upon the number of 'outs' a player's hand has. Outs are simply the number of unseen cards which will improve a player's hand – in other words, the cards which are still in the deck. But, many newcomers often ask, 'What about the cards that my opponents might hold?'

It's a reasonable question, but the cards of all your opponents should be disregarded because there is absolutely no way of knowing for sure what they are. It is the same for all of the other players as well. In the end, the pot odds can be seen as a measure of probability and so cannot account for the unseen cards.

Incidentally, before examining the table, let's look at an example of an out.

Player holds   **The flop produces**

The player now has four cards of the same suit (hearts). This is known as a flush draw. This player believes (with good reason) that a King flush would win them the pot. Because there are nine hearts still left in the deck – remember, the unseen cards already in play are ignored – the player therefore has nine 'outs'. Look at the table that follows to see how nine outs translate to odds of 4/1 (outcome odds) against completing a flush on the turn or the river. Therefore, if the **pot odds** were 4/1 or better it would be worthwhile continuing.

Odds of completing a hand on the turn or the river

Outs if you have ...	and are drawing to ...	Outcome odds
1 Three of a Kind Inside Straight Flush Draw	Four of a Kind Straight Flush	46/1
2 Pair Open-ended Straight Flush Draw	Three of a Kind Straight Flush	23/1
3 Over card (1 high hole-card)	Pair	15/1
4 Two Pairs **Inside Straight Draw**	Full House **Straight**	11/1
5 Pair	Two Pairs or Three of a Kind	8/1
6 **Over cards (2 high hole-cards)**	**Pair**	7/1
7 Three of a Kind	Full House or Four of a Kind	6/1
8 **Open-ended Straight Draw**	**Straight**	5/1
9 **Flush Draw**	**Flush**	4/1
12 Inside Straight Flush Draw	Straight Flush, Flush or Straight	3/1
15 Open-ended Straight Flush Draw	Straight Flush, Flush or Straight	2/1

(The hands **in bold** are the most common instances where players will need to calculate the pot odds.)

It should also be noted that the table contains the terms 'Inside Straight Draw', 'Over cards', 'Open-ended Straight Draw' and 'Flush Draw'. By now you may already know what is meant by these terms, but let's take a quick look at their definitions to make sure.

Inside Straight Draw: A set of cards which require a specific card to fit in between them to make a straight. So, if a player holds a 5, 7 as their hole-cards and the flop has brought Ace, 8, 9 they will need a 6 to come out on the turn or the river to give them a straight.

Over cards: The term used when hole-cards are of higher value than the community cards already in play. For example, a player holding a pair of Aces has a higher value hand than a flop which has produced 10, 7 and 6.

Open-ended Straight Draw: A set of cards where a card either end of what a player already has will give them a straight. For example, if a player holds 7, 6 and the flop brings Ace, 8, 9, they can complete a straight if the turn or the river brings either a 10 or a 5 (they would then have either 6, 7, 8, 9, 10 or 5, 6, 7, 8, 9).

Flush Draw: Where the turn or the river card might give a player five cards of the same suit.

Using the table, all that needs to be done is to compare the pot odds against the outcome odds. When the former is higher than the latter, a player should continue to bet. Put at its most simple, it's the same reasoning behind the fact that you should always bet if anyone ever offers you odds of 6/4 about calling correctly on the toss of a coin. Calling correctly on the toss of a coin is 1/1, so if you can obtain 6/4 you must win in the long run.

Note that there are also pot odds to be considered against completing a three-card straight or flush draw. But in these instances to complete the hand you will need the perfect cards on both the turn and the river. The odds here are a minimum of 23/1, with one possibility being as high as 71/1. In these instances it is very unlikely the pot will be high enough to justify the odds against winning.

The Turn

In a lot of Texas Hold 'em games, or at least ones which are being contested by players who know what they are doing, there is only a small amount of betting action after the fourth community card is revealed. Generally, a good poker player will adopt a cautious approach after the turn because this is when an over-aggressive bet could frighten off players who might otherwise go through to the river.

Also, here is where good players watch out for possible flushes. This is mostly the case when the flop has produced two cards of the same suit and the turn then produces a third. When this happens, any player who does not yet hold a flush must remember that there is now a reasonable chance of at least one of their opponents having one. In these cases the player without the flush would need to be drawing to a pretty big hand to have any real chance.

They should also be aware of how their opponents are betting because that can yield a lot of clues. Anyone checking at this point might be simply having a free look, **or might be trying to induce others to think they have a weak hand in the hope that their opponents bet through to the river (this is known as 'trapping').**

Of course, looking back at the most recent example (where the player held the A ♥, 5 ♥ as their hole-cards) all the players left in, regardless of whether they checked or bet, will have had equal reason to suspect that one of their opponents was close to a flush, given the cards on the flop. This is the beauty of poker. Whether it is played in real life or on the internet, over time any player who can make the right decision in these kinds of situations will make a profit regardless of whether they are short-term lucky with the cards or not. **But the key to making the right decisions is playing correctly from the hole-cards onwards.** However, in the example there was another possibility to consider.

Supposing after the turn card a player had already been sitting on a flush and their opponent(s) checked. These opponents could have been taking it easy so as not to frighten the others off, or they could have been trying to take a free look at what happened next. Either way, the player holding the flush would have needed to remember what was said earlier. If they had bet over-aggressively at this point their good hand might not have received the reward it deserved because at least some of the other players who were possibly trying to have a free look (due to the fact they were holding weak hands) will have almost certainly folded. So, the player with the flush may well have done best to also check and await the river before then going for the jugular. That is unless they knew their opponents through having previously taken notes about them.

If their notes suggested that some of their opponents were reckless – and the internet is full of reckless players – the player may have wanted to bet up their strong hand in order to draw more money into the pot from those playing a loose game. (This is why we will be covering note-taking in chapter 11.)

The River

As you know, the final community card is called the river. The river card can completely turn a hand around and subsequently cause some fireworks in the last round of betting. But by now a good poker player will either have an excellent chance of scooping the pot, or will have previously folded poor cards. Other than pulling off the occasional outrageous bluff, or having equally outrageous fortune on the last card, loose players who chance their arm with weak hands all the way through to the river will not last long at the online poker tables.

The river is when no-limit games really get down to the nitty-gritty, especially in tournaments. This is because the players left in will often try to 'blast' their opponents out of the pot with a big bet.

7

Hand Analysis and Play Analysis

L et's now try to pull together what we have looked at so far by analysing some fictional Texas Hold 'em hands in action. They are fairly simple examples which newcomers should find pretty easy to follow.

Note that all of the hands have been broken down to show what each player was actually holding, and for some of them a table is included charting the course of play, followed then by a detailed analysis.

The hands are described in the past tense with position 10 being the viewpoint from which each hand is primarily analysed. Where any recommendations are made, please remember that they are based upon the author's personal view of how a newcomer should play poker. These may not always be the most popular, or in some cases even the most accepted, ways!

In all instances there are ten players taking part in the hand, and the positions they occupy have been named simply as 1, 2, 3, 4, 5, 6, 7, 8, 9 and 10. The game is limit £10 / £20 with £10 as the small blind and £20 as the big one. There are a maximum of three raises allowed per betting round.

Hand One

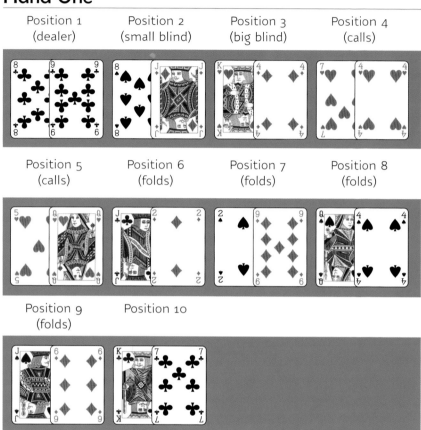

Position 1 (dealer)	Position 2 (small blind)	Position 3 (big blind)	Position 4 (calls)
Position 5 (calls)	Position 6 (folds)	Position 7 (folds)	Position 8 (folds)
Position 9 (folds)	Position 10		

By the time position 10 had to act, five other players were still in: positions 1 (dealer), 2 (small blind), 3 (big blind), 4 and 5.

For position 10, this first appeared to be a hand possibly to go with in the hope of drawing to a flush. Indeed, according to one of the tables in the last chapter, these cards could have been considered playable. But the recommendation this time was to **fold** because four other players had still to act. Yes, up to that point only two players had acted (and then had only called), but position 10's hole-cards were not strong. Perhaps with only three opponents left it might have been worth going to the flop, but a minimum of five remaining live hands spelt danger.

Folding hands like this will save newcomers cash in the long run. For example, a big weakness in position 10's hole-cards was that if a King had come through on the flop to give them a pair, the kicker would only have been a 7.

Hand Two

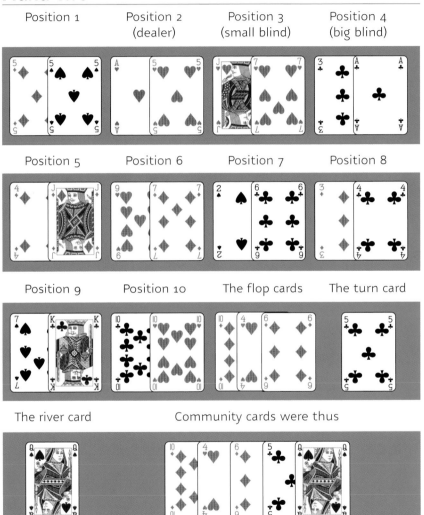

Position 1	Position 2 (dealer)	Position 3 (small blind)	Position 4 (big blind)

Position 5	Position 6	Position 7	Position 8

Position 9	Position 10	The flop cards	The turn card

The river card	Community cards were thus

Let's chart the progress of this hand in more detail:

Key
R1 = Betting Round 1   R2 = Betting Round 2   D = Dealer
SB = Small Blind   BB = Big Blind   FD = Fold
CA = Call   B = Bet   RA = Raise
CH = Check   RR = Re-raise
* = first to act (putting in the blinds counts as an action)

POSITION	THE FLOP			THE TURN			THE RIVER		
	R1 £ R2 £	R1	£ R2	£	R1	£ R2	£	R1	£ R2	£
1	FD – – –	–	– –	–	–	– –	–	–	– –	–
2(D)	CA 40 FD –	–	– –	–	–	– –	–	–	– –	–
3*	SB 10 FD –	–	– –	–	–	– –	–	–	– –	–
4	BB 20 CA 20	CH	– CA	20	CH	– CA	40	CH	– CA	20
5	FD – – –	–	– –	–	–	– –	–	–	– –	–
6	CA 20 CA 20	CH	– CA	20	CH	– CA	40	CH	– CA	20
7	FD – – –	–	– –	–	–	– –	–	–	– –	–
8	FD – – –	–	– –	–	–	– –	–	–	– –	–
9	FD – – –	–	– –	–	–	– –	–	–	– –	–
10	RA 20 – –	B	20 –	–	B	40 –	–	B	20 –	–

Play Analysis

Hole-Cards

Round 1

After the deal, position 5 folded, position 6 called the big blind, and positions 7, 8 and 9 all folded. The action then came to position 10. Being in a late betting position, the player had a good hand with their pair of 10s. Hence, the correct play was to **raise** the stakes. Position 2 then ended the betting round with a call.

Round 2

It was down to the player nearest to the dealer's left to act first. This was position 3. They folded. Position 4 called, as did position 6. Their actions meant that the pot was equalised and so the betting interval ended.

The Flop

(Position 10 now had three 10s – a strong hand.)

Round 1

Position 4 was now the first to act and they checked. Position 6 did the same. This brought the betting to position 10. The correct play was to make a **bet**, as three 10s against only two players was pretty reasonable! The flop had meant that one of those two players needed to be drawing to a straight or better, or to a higher trips, to beat position 10 (to be drawing to a higher trips they needed to be already holding a pair of Jacks or better with their hole-cards).

Round 2

Players 4 and 6 both called to equalise the pot.

The Turn

Round 1

Position 4 was still first to act and they checked, as did position 6. This may have been a pointer to them having weak hands so the correct course of action for position 10 was to make a further bet.

Round 2

Positions 4 and 6 called to equalise the pot (note that neither of them raised).

The River

Round 1

Positions 4 and 6 checked. Correct play for position 10 was to make yet another bet.

The Showdown

At the showdown, position 10 won with their three 10s. An interesting question here is: Should they have made a bigger bet on the river card? This is very much open to debate, but for the newcomer the approach should fundamentally be a cautious one. Anyway, had they made a bigger bet they may have caused one, or both, of their two remaining opponents to fold. Perhaps position 10's course of action was a little cautious, but betting conundrums such as this really do illustrate the beauty of poker.

Hand 3

Position 1	Position 2	Position 3 (dealer)	Position 4 (small blind)

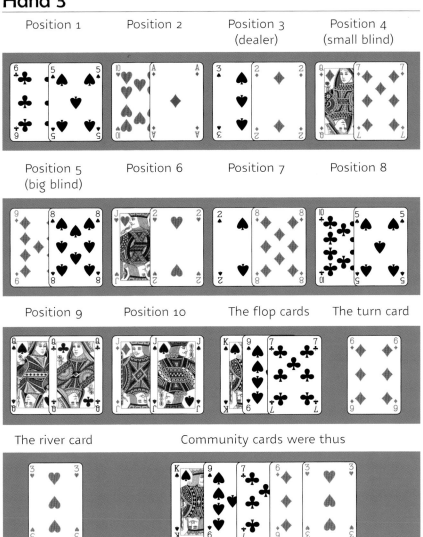

Position 5 (big blind)	Position 6	Position 7	Position 8

Position 9	Position 10	The flop cards	The turn card

The river card	Community cards were thus

Let's assume that position 10 played this hand as well.

Key R1 = Betting Round 1   R2 = Betting Round 2   D = Dealer
 SB = Small Blind   BB = Big Blind   FD = Fold
 CA = Call   B = Bet   RA = Raise
 CH = Check   RR = Re-raise
 * = first to act (putting in the blinds counts as an action)

POSITION		THE FLOP				THE TURN				THE RIVER			
	R1	**£**	**R2**	**£**	**R1**	**£**	**R2**	**£**	**R1**	**£**	**R2**	**£**	
1	FD	–	–	–	–	–	–	–	–	–	–	–	–	–
2	CA	40	–	–	FD	–	–	–	–	–	–	–	–	–
3(D)	FD	–	–	–	–	–	–	–	–	–	–	–	–	–
4 *	SB	10	CA	30	B	20	–	–	B	40	–	–	CH	–	–	–
5	BB	20	CA	20	CA	20	–	–	CA	40	–	–	CH	–	–	–
6	FD	–	–	–	–	–	–	–	–	–	–	–	–	–
7	FD	–	–	–	–	–	–	–	–	–	–	–	–	–
8	FD	–	–	–	–	–	–	–	–	–	–	–	–	–
9	RA	20	–	–	CA	20	–	–	CA	40	–	–	CH	–	–	–
10	CA	40	–	–	CA	20	–	–	FD	–	–	–	–	–	–	–

Play Analysis

Hole-Cards

Round 1

After the deal, positions 6, 7 and 8 folded. Position 9 raised the big blind and it was then position 10 to act. A pair of Jacks looked quite good so the **call** was correct, although some may have gone with a re-raise. Position 1 folded, position 2 called and position 3 folded to end the betting round.

Round 2

Position 4 (the small blind) was now 'under the gun'. They called. Position 5 also called to equalise the pot.

The Flop

Round 1

Position 4 was still the first to act and they made a bet. Position 5 called, as did position 9. This brought the action back to position 10. At this point they began to appreciate how their pair of Jacks might not look quite so good now. The flop had brought a King and so anyone holding another of those in their hole-cards would have been beating them. Also, both the blinds had continued. But their pair of Jacks was still worth making a **call** with. This equalised the pot.

The Turn

Round 1

Position 4 had to act first and did so with another bet. Position 5 called the bet, as did position 9. It was up to position 10 again, but the recommendation was to **fold**. The turn had done nothing for position 10 and, with three other players left in, the pair of Jacks now looked weak.

The River

Round 1

Positions 4, 5 and 9 all checked.

The Showdown

At the showdown, position 9 won with a pair of Queens. This beat position 4 who had a pair of 7s, and position 5 who had a pair of 9s. In the end, position 10 would not have been too far off, and perhaps a bit of bluffing would have scared away position 9, but remember that they were defending their blind so they may not have gone away too easily. Another example of the nuances of poker!

Hand 4

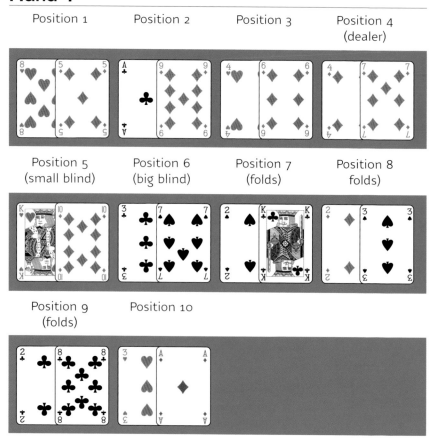

Position 1	Position 2	Position 3	Position 4 (dealer)

Position 5 (small blind)	Position 6 (big blind)	Position 7 (folds)	Position 8 folds)

Position 9 (folds)	Position 10

No point going on to look at the flop, turn and river here. Two things came together to give position 10 only one realistic course of action. Their Ace was okay but its kicker was only a 3. Combining this with the fact that they would have been in an early betting position given that positions 7, 8 and 9 had all folded, meant they were left with no choice other than to **fold**.

Hand 5

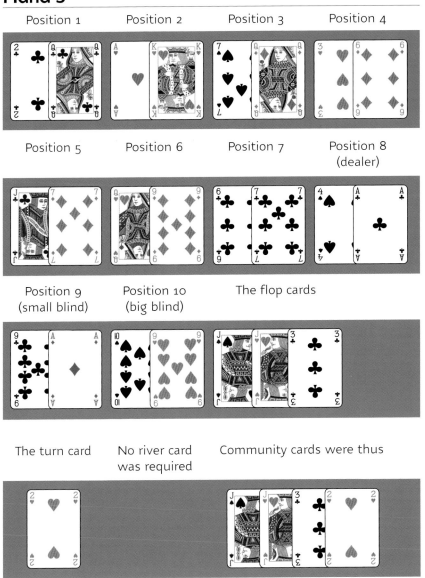

Position 1 Position 2 Position 3 Position 4

Position 5 Position 6 Position 7 Position 8 (dealer)

Position 9 (small blind) Position 10 (big blind) The flop cards

The turn card No river card was required Community cards were thus

Key R1 = Betting Round 1   R2 = Betting Round 2   D = Dealer
     SB = Small Blind   BB = Big Blind   FD = Fold
     CA = Call   B = Bet   RA = Raise
     CH = Check   RR = Re-raise
     * = first to act (putting in the blinds counts as an action)

P O S I T I O N	THE FLOP				THE TURN				THE RIVER			
	R1	**£**	**R2**	**£**	**R1**	**£**	**R2**	**£**	**R1**	**£**	**R2**	**£**
1	FD	–	–	–	–	–	–	–	–	–	–	–
2	RA	20	–	–	B	20	–	–	B	20	–	–
3	FD	–	–	–	–	–	–	–	–	–	–	–
4	FD	–	–	–	–	–	–	–	–	–	–	–
5	FD	–	–	–	–	–	–	–	–	–	–	–
6	CA	40	–	–	FD	–	–	–	–	–	–	–
7	FD	–	–	–	–	–	–	–	–	–	–	–
8(D)	FD	–	–	–	–	–	–	–	–	–	–	–
9*	SB	10	CA	30	CH	–	CA	20	CH	FD	–	–
10	BB	20	CA	20	CH	–	FD	–	–	–	–	–

Play Analysis

Hole-Cards

Round 1
Position 10 was in the big blind position. In the first round of betting, position 2 raised the big blind, position 6 called and all the other positions folded.

Round 2
Position 9 (the small blind) was now under the gun. They called. It was then up to position 10 to act. Their non-suited 9 and 10 was a drawing hand so the recommendation was to **call**, but also to keep a wary eye on position 2 who had raised from an early position. Position 10's call equalised the pot.

The Flop

Round 1 and Round 2
The flop meant that position 10 still had the chance of a straight in three ways, but the right cards were going to be required on the turn and the river (they needed a 7 and an 8, or an 8 and a Q, or a Q and a K). They certainly had a chance but, after position 9 checked, the recommendation was to do the same, not least because position 2 had made a raise so early on (caution again being the byword).

    After position 10 had **checked,** position 2 bet, position 6 folded and position 9 called. The action was back to position 10. The recommendation was now to **fold.** Yes, it may have been tempting to carry on but position 10 had nothing and was hoping that the turn and the river would sort them out. Chances are that the other two players (positions 2 and 9) already had nice hands and so discretion was the better part of valour here.

The Turn

Round 1
Position 9 was the first to act and they checked. Position 2 continued their strong play with a bet. This was enough for position 9 who folded, thus meaning the river card was not required.

The Showdown

As everyone had folded, position 2 won the pot, effectively with these hole-cards:

After the flop and the turn, they were one card away from an Ace flush. With a suited Ace and King as their hole-cards it was clear why they kept betting, but perhaps position 9 was being optimistic by continuing with an non-suited Ace, 9! Still, the day someone opens a shop selling hindsight everyone else can stop playing poker!

Incidentally, position 10 played their hand better than position 9 because they went through to the flop, but didn't spend any money afterwards. However, position 9 had one last call before the fourth card.

Hand 6

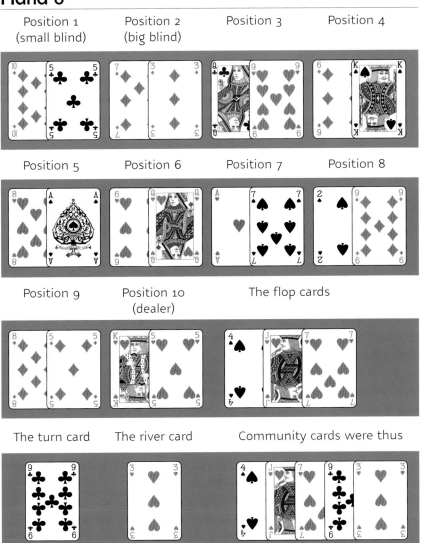

| Position 1 (small blind) | Position 2 (big blind) | Position 3 | Position 4 |

| Position 5 | Position 6 | Position 7 | Position 8 |

| Position 9 | Position 10 (dealer) | The flop cards |

| The turn card | The river card | Community cards were thus |

Key
R1 = Betting Round 1   R2 = Betting Round 2   D = Dealer
SB = Small Blind   BB = Big Blind   FD = Fold
CA = Call   B = Bet   RA = Raise
CH = Check   RR = Re-raise
* = first to act (putting in the blinds counts as an action)

POSITION	THE FLOP			THE TURN			THE RIVER			
	R1 £ R2 £	R1 £ R2 £		R1 £ R2 £		R1 £ R2 £
1*	SB 10 FD —	— — — —	— — — —	B 40 FD —
2	BB 20 CH —	CH — CA 20	CH — — —	B 40 FD —
3	FD — — —	— — — —	— — — —	— — — —
4	FD — — —	— — — —	— — — —	— — — —
5	CA 20 — —	CH — CA 20	CH — — —	FD — — —
6	CA 20 — —	CH — CA 20	CH — — —	RA 80 CA 40
7	CA 20 — —	CH — CA 20	CH — — —	FD — — —
8	FD — — —	— — — —	— — — —	— — — —
9	CA 20 — —	CH — CA 20	CH — — —	FD — — —
10(D)	CA 20 — —	B 20 — —	CH — — —	RR 120 — —

Play Analysis

Hole-Cards

Round 1

Position 10 was the 'dealer', the best position of all with regard to the betting. Positions 1 and 2 were the blinds. Positions 3 and 4 both folded. Positions 5, 6 and 7 all called. Position 8 folded, but 9 called. This left position 10 to act. Their choice was to **call**, which was the recommended action, not so much because they had King, 5 suited, but more because they were in the best betting position.

Round 2

Position 1 folded. Position 2 then checked, as did everyone else. This equalised the pot and the betting interval ended.

The Flop

Round 1

The two hearts on the flop now gave position 10 a reasonable chance of obtaining a flush.

   Position 2 was the first to act and they checked, as did positions 5, 6, 7 and 9. This left position 10 to act. The strong recommendation was to make a **bet**. This is because the odds of making a flush by the river card were 1.9/1. Furthermore, the pot odds were 5.3/1. (See shortly for the out odds and the pot odds for this hand.)

Round 2

Position 2 was still the first to act and they called. All the remaining players did the same thing to equalise the pot.

The Turn

Round 1

After the turn all the other players checked. The recommendation was for position 10 to do the same thing. This was because they had not yet obtained the correct card to hold a flush, and also because a lot of other players were still in the hand.

The River

The final community card came out as

This was great news for position 10, as they were now holding a flush.

Round 1

Position 2 was again the first to act. They made a bet. This was enough to force position 5 to fold. Position 6 raised. Positions 7 and 9 both folded. This left position 10 to act. Interestingly enough, position 10 was able to see that from **their** hole-cards plus the cards on the board only **one** of the two players left in could beat them.

Position 10 held a King flush (hearts). Given the community cards, a flush (hearts) was the highest hand possible and so only if one of the two other players held an A ♥ would position 10 be defeated. Because, at worst, position 10 held the second highest hand, they knew that they had beaten at least one of the other two players. Hence, the correct course of action was to re-raise.

Round 2

Position 2 folded and position 6 called to equalise the pot.

The Showdown

Position 10 won the pot with their flush: K ♥, J ♥, 7 ♥, 5 ♥, 3 ♥.

It was a good pot to win because three players went through to the river. This is a significant hand for a newcomer to note. Aided by being in the last betting position, position 10 played fairly aggressively (they made a bet straight after the flop, then re-raised on the river) and was rewarded by the river card bringing them a flush.

Outcome Odds / Pot Odds

Because position 10 went to the river with a number of other players, it is worth looking at the outcome odds / pot odds as the hand developed.

Let's first look at the odds before the flop. Remember, position 10 had K ♥, 5 ♥ as their hole-cards.

Odds against the flop giving position 10 three Kings or three 5s	73/1
Odds against the flop giving position 10 two pairs: Kings and 5s	48/1
Odds against the flop giving position 10 a pair of Kings	6.4/1
Odds against the flop giving position 10 a pair of 5s	6.4/1
Odds against position 10 obtaining a five-card flush (hearts)	118/1
Pot odds at this point	**5.3/1**

Here it is only academic that the pot odds were less than the chances of obtaining the better hands. In this case the pot odds only really become relevant after the flop.

After the Flop

Odds against position 10 obtaining a flush (hearts) by the turn	4.2/1
Odds against position 10 obtaining a flush (hearts) by the river	1.9/1
Odds against position 10 obtaining a pair of Kings by the turn	14.7/1
Odds against position 10 obtaining a pair of Kings by the river	13.9/1
Odds against position 10 obtaining a pair of 5s by the turn	14.7/1
Odds against position 10 obtaining a pair of 5s by the river	13.9/1
Pot odds at this point	**6.3/1**

Here you can see that there was considerable value in position 10 continuing to bet. With pot odds of just over 6/1, against odds of either 1.9/1 or 4.2/1 against obtaining the hand which they believed would win, they had no choice but to continue.

After the Turn

Odds against position 10 obtaining a flush (hearts) by the river	4.1/1
Odds against position 10 obtaining a pair of Kings by the river	14.4/1
Odds against position 10 obtaining a pair of 5s by the river	14.4/1
Pot odds at this point	**6.2/1**

Again, the pot odds amply illustrate why it was worthwhile position 10 continuing after the fourth card.

Hand 7

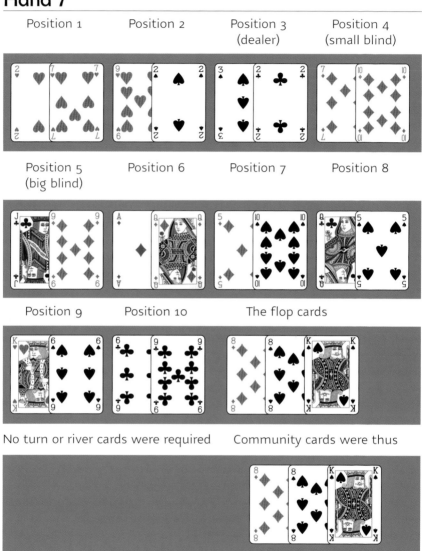

| Position 1 | Position 2 | Position 3 (dealer) | Position 4 (small blind) |

| Position 5 (big blind) | Position 6 | Position 7 | Position 8 |

| Position 9 | Position 10 | The flop cards |

No turn or river cards were required   Community cards were thus

Key R1 = Betting Round 1   R2 = Betting Round 2   D = Dealer
SB = Small Blind   BB = Big Blind   FD = Fold
CA = Call   B = Bet   RA = Raise
CH = Check   RR = Re-raise
* = first to act (putting in the blinds counts as an action)

POSITION		THE FLOP			THE TURN			THE RIVER			
	R1	**£**	**R2**	**£**	**R1**	**£**	**R2**	**£**	**R1**	**£**	**R2**	**£**
1	FD	–	–	–	–	–	–	–	–	–	–	–
2	FD	–	–	–	–	–	–	–	–	–	–	–
3(D)	FD	–	–	–	–	–	–	–	–	–	–	–
4*	SB	10	CA	30	CH	–	FD	–	–	–	–	–
5	BB	20	CA	20	CH	–	FD	–	–	–	–	–
6	RA	20	–	–	B	20	–	–	–	–	–	–
7	FD	–	–	–	–	–	–	–	–	–	–	–
8	FD	–	–	–	–	–	–	–	–	–	–	–
9	FD	–	–	–	–	–	–	–	–	–	–	–
10	FD	–	–	–	–	–	–	–	–	–	–	–

Play Analysis

This hand has been included to illustrate how some players vigorously defend their blinds, and also to show another example of why a good player will fold poor hole-cards.

Hole-Cards

Round 1

After the blinds (positions 4 and 5), position 6 raised. This was an early position to raise from and was probably an indication of the strength of position 6's hand. This is a good example of how note-taking during a game can be of assistance. If during the game any of the other players had already noted that position 6 was someone who quickly raised when they had a good hand, they would have been wary about continuing. After position 6 had raised, positions 7, 8 and 9 all folded. This brought the action to position 10.

Position 10's hand of 6 ♣, 9 ♣ was not enough to continue with, given their medium position in the betting. Thus, the recommendation was to **fold**. After position 10 folded, positions 1 and 2 both folded before both the blinds called to equalise the pot.

The Flop

Round 1

Position 4 was first to act and they checked, as did position 5. This opened the way for position 6 who made a bet.

Round 2

Positions 4 and 5 folded to leave the pot for position 6 without the need for either the turn or the river cards.

Result

Position 6 won the pot because everyone else folded. There are three things to note from this hand. First, position 6 possibly raised a little too early. With a suited Ace and Queen they probably should have gone steadier and tried to keep some more players in the pot with them. (Remember, a player with a good hand needs to force at least some of the other players to fold, but must also allow those holding the second- and third-best hands to continue in the pot.)

Second, at least one of the two blinds played on when they should not have done so. Okay, position 4 did have a suited 7 and 10 but position 5 was in quite poor shape with their non-suited Jack and 9.

More importantly, both blinds should have also appreciated how quickly position 6 actually made their raise. You can just about forgive position 4 for calling up to the flop, but possibly not position 5.

After the flop, position 4 could still have achieved a straight or a flush, while position 5 could still have achieved the former. However, whether it was wise for both positions to make a call to the fresh bet of position 6 is debatable. Another point to note about the blinds players was that, after the flop, they first checked. Seeing as position 6 had already made a very early raise before the flop, they were probably playing into position 6's hands by advertising their timidity.

The third point to note is that had position 10 continued they would have seen the flop give them three 8s. Such is the frustration of poker.

Hand 8

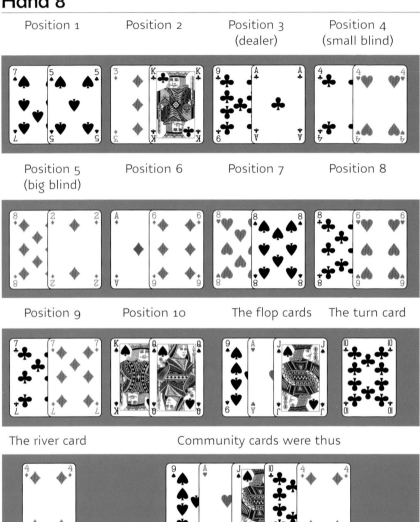

Position 1   Position 2   Position 3 (dealer)   Position 4 (small blind)

Position 5 (big blind)   Position 6   Position 7   Position 8

Position 9   Position 10   The flop cards   The turn card

The river card   Community cards were thus

Key R1 = Betting Round 1 R2 = Betting Round 2 D = Dealer
SB = Small Blind BB = Big Blind FD = Fold
CA = Call B = Bet RA = Raise
CH = Check RR = Re-raise
* = first to act (putting in the blinds counts as an action)

POSITION					THE FLOP				THE TURN				THE RIVER			
	R1	£	R2	£	R1	£	R2	£	R1	£	R2	£	R1	£	R2	£
1	FD	–	–	–	–	–	–	–	–	–	–	–	–	–	–	–
2	FD	–	–	–	–	–	–	–	–	–	–	–	–	–	–	–
3(D)	RA	20	–	–	RA	20	–	–	CA	40	–	–	CA	40	–	–
4*	SB	10	CA	30	B	20	CA	20	CH	–	FD	–	–	–	–	–
5	BB	20	CA	20	FD	–	–	–	–	–	–	–	–	–	–	–
6	FD	–	–	–	–	–	–	–	–	–	–	–	–	–	–	–
7	CA	20	CA	20	FD	–	–	–	–	–	–	–	–	–	–	–
8	FD	–	–	–	–	–	–	–	–	–	–	–	–	–	–	–
9	CA	20	CA	20	CA	20	FD	–	–	–	–	–	–	–	–	–
10	CA	20	CA	20	CA	20	CA	20	B	40	–	–	B	40	–	–

Play Analysis

Hole-Cards

Round 1

After the blinds, position 6 folded but position 7 (pair of 8s) called. Position 8 folded, but position 9 called with their pair of 7s. This brought the action to position 10 and they **called**. With two high, suited hole-cards it was correct to remain in, but also probably correct to **call** rather than do anything stronger. After position 10 acted, positions 1 and 2 folded but position 3 raised with their suited Ace, 9 (clubs).

Round 2
Position 4 (the small blind) called with their pair of 4s. Position 5 did the same with their 8, 2 suited (diamonds). Positions 7 and 9 **called** to again bring the action to position 10. The correct action was to **call**. This equalised the pot and set up what was looking to be a big hand.

The Flop

Round 1
Position 4 kicked things off with a bet although the flop had not improved their hand. Positions 5 and 7 both folded. However, position 9 continued with a call despite the flop not helping them either. The action came back to position 10.

The flop had brought 9 ♠, A ♥, J ♠. This was good news for position 10 because they already had K ♠, Q ♠. The potential in the hand was clear to see. The 10 ♠ on either the turn or the river would have given them the second-best straight flush possible. But any other spade would have still given them a flush. Furthermore, any 10 would have given them the best possible straight. This gave them a total of 12 outs – three 10s and nine spades. The strong recommendation was to continue with a call. The only reason it was a **call**, as opposed to a raise, was because there were still three other players left in and, as at that point, position 10 did not yet have a hand.

After the call from position 10, position 3 raised, their hand having improved to two pairs, Aces and 9s.

Round 2
Position 4 now called, which induced a fold from position 9. The action was back with position 10. Again, the recommendation was to **call**. Given the pot odds, reproduced for this hand a bit later on, a raise would not have been out of the question either. But, again, for a newcomer caution should be the watchword, so the recommendation was a call. This equalised the pot.

The Turn

Round 1
It was down to just positions 3, 4 and 10. Position 4 was the first to act and they checked – possibly their first sign of weakness? This brought the action to position 10. Seeing as the turn had produced a 10 ♣ they

were now in possession of the highest possible straight. Therefore, the recommendation was for them to make a **bet**. In response to this position 3 called.

Round 2
Position 4, whom the turn had not helped, folded, which left positions 3 and 10 to see the river card.

The River
Round 1
Position 10 was now the first to act because position 3 was holding the dealer's disc. The river had done nothing for position 10, but they already had a sizzling hand. Hence, the correct action was to make a **bet**. Position 3 called to equalise the pot.

The Showdown

Position 10 won with their straight. Position 3 had two pairs, Aces and 9s, but position 10's A, K, Q, J, 10 was clearly enough to take the money.

Pot Odds

Let's look at the pot odds for this hand. We'll start with the odds on the flop.

Odds on the Flop

Odds against position 10 making a flush (spades) on the turn	4.2/1
Odds against position 10 making a flush (spades) by the river	1.9/1
Odds against position 10 making a straight on the turn	14.6/1
Odds against position 10 making a straight by the river	9/1
Odds against position 10 making a pair of Kings on the turn	14.7/1
Odds against position 10 making a pair of Kings by the river	16.2/1
Odds against position 10 making a pair of Queens on the turn	14.7/1
Odds against position 10 making a pair of Queens by the river	16.2/1
Pot odds	**13.9/1**

Odds on the Turn

Remember, at this point position 10 had made a straight.

Odds against position 10 making a flush (spades) by the river   4.1/1

Pot odds   **9.4/1**

Hand 9

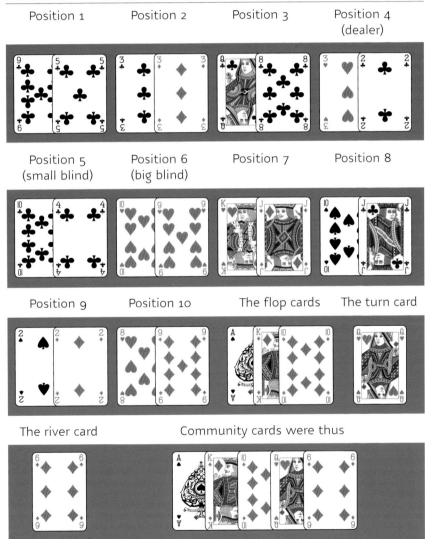

Position 1   Position 2   Position 3   Position 4 (dealer)

Position 5 (small blind)   Position 6 (big blind)   Position 7   Position 8

Position 9   Position 10   The flop cards   The turn card

The river card   Community cards were thus

Key R1 = Betting Round 1 R2 = Betting Round 2 D = Dealer
     SB = Small Blind   BB = Big Blind   FD = Fold
     CA = Call   B = Bet   RA = Raise
     CH = Check   RR = Re-raise
     * = first to act (putting in the blinds counts as an action)

POSITION	R1	£	R2	£	THE FLOP R1	£	R2	£	THE TURN R1	£	R2	£	THE RIVER R1	£	R2	£
1	FD	–	–	–	–	–	–	–	–	–	–	–	–	–	–	–
2	CA	20	CA	40	B	20	–	–	FD	–	–	–	–	–	–	–
3	CA	20	CA	40	CA	20	–	–	FD	–	–	–	–	–	–	–
4(D)	FD	–	–	–	–	–	–	–	–	–	–	–	–	–	–	–
5*	SB	10	FD	–	–	–	–	–	–	–	–	–	–	–	–	–
6	BB	20	RA	20	CH	–	FD	–	–	–	–	–	–	–	–	–
7	CA	20	CA	40	CH	–	CA	20	B	20	–	–	B	20	CA	20
8	CA	20	CA	40	CH	–	CA	20	CA	20	–	–	RA	20	–	–
9	CA	20	CA	40	CH	–	FD	–	–	–	–	–	–	–	–	–
10	CA	20	CA	40	FD	–	–	–	–	–	–	–	–	–	–	–

Play Analysis

Hole-Cards

Round 1

After the blinds, position 7 called with their non-suited King and Jack. Position 8, with their non-suited Jack and 10, also called. Position 9 did the same thing with their pair of 2s. The action came to position 10. It's possibly open to debate, but the correct action with the connected 8, 9 was a **call**. After the call from position 10, position 1 folded, but position 2 with their pair of 3s called. Position 3 (suited Q, 8) did the same thing but position 4, with their non-suited 3 and 2, folded.

Round 2

Position 5 (the small blind) folded. Position 6 (the big blind) raised with their 10, 9 suited. Positions 7, 8 and 9 all called. Position 10 was next to act. There were a lot of players heading for the flop, but the correct action was to stay in the hand by **calling**. After this, positions 2 and 3 called.

The Flop

Round 1

Position 6 (a pair of 10s), position 7 (a pair of Kings), position 8 (another pair of 10s) and position 9 (remained on a pair of 2s) all checked. The action was with position 10 again. The flop had given them nothing and they wisely folded. They had nothing and one of the other players may well have already flopped into a big straight. What made it worse, not that they knew it, was that so many other cards could have still come out on the turn or the river that might have beaten them (position 10) down further. In fact, there were 21 cards that could have beaten them on the turn or the river, even if they were not beaten already. Clearly, the best course of action was to do what they did. After position 10 folded, position 2 bet and then position 3 called.

Round 2

Position 6 folded. Positions 7 and 8 called. Position 9 folded.

The Turn

Round 1

At the turn, positions 2, 3, 7 and 8 were still left in. Position 7 was now under the gun and they made a bet because the fourth community card had given them the highest straight. The same thing had happened to position 8, but they only called, sensing that position 7 may have hit the same hand. Positions 2 and 3 folded, realising that the board was pointing towards a straight having been created.

The River

Round 1

Position 7 was the first to act and they made a bet. After the river card, position 8 realised that they probably had at least the equal of position 7 so they raised.

Round 2

Position 7 equalised the pot with a call. So, the showdown was between positions 7 and 8.

The Showdown

After all that, positions 7 and 8 had to split the pot because they had tied hands. Poker sometimes produces deals like these where players go through to the end stages with identical hands.

Hand 10

For the final breakdown of a Texas Hold 'em hand, let's do things a bit differently. This time it's a hand from a real-life game that took place on TV not so very long ago. There were only five players. Instead of position 10, this time let's look at the hand from the viewpoint of position 5.

The game was £5 / £10 with the small blind being £2 and the big blind £4. There was a minimum bet or raise of £5. For the first interval of betting the maximum bet or raise was £10, but for the other intervals it was £30.

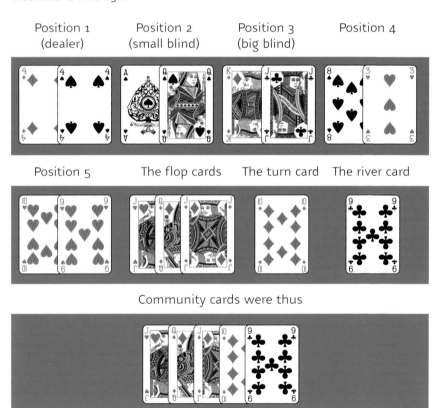

Position 1 (dealer)	Position 2 (small blind)	Position 3 (big blind)	Position 4

| Position 5 | The flop cards | The turn card | The river card |

Community cards were thus

Let's see how things progressed.

Key R1 = Betting Round 1   R2 = Betting Round 2   D = Dealer
SB = Small Blind   BB = Big Blind   FD = Fold
CA = Call   B = Bet   RA = Raise
CH = Check   RR = Re-raise
* = first to act (putting in the blinds counts as an action)

POSITION					THE FLOP				THE TURN				THE RIVER			
	R1	£	R2	£	R1	£	R2	£	R1	£	R2	£	R1	£	R2	£
1(D)	CA	4	–	–	CA	10	–	–	FD	–	–	–	–	–	–	–
2*	SB	2	CA	2	B	10	–	–	CH	–	CA	30	CH	–	–	–
3	BB	4	–	–	CA	10	–	–	B	30	–	–	CH	–	–	–
4	FD	–	–	–	–	–	–	–	–	–	–	–	–	–	–	–
5	CA	4	–	–	CA	10	–	–	CA	30	–	–	CH	–	–	–

Play Analysis

Hole-Cards

Round 1

1   After the blinds (£2 and £4) from positions 2 and 3, position 4 was the first to act. With two non-suited cards, the highest of which was an 8, they quickly folded.

2   Position 5 had 9 ♥, 10 ♥. These were hole-cards worth calling with (£4).

3   Position 1 had a small pair. They also called for the £4.

The pot now contained £14.

Round 2

1   Position 2 had a suited Ace and Queen. Having already put in the small blind of £2, they called the last bet with another £2. This equalised the pot.

At this point the pot contained £16.

The Flop

The flop did wonders for player 3 who went to three Jacks.

Round 1

1   Position 2 was under the gun. With a hand of two pairs, Queens and Jacks, they could not now obtain a flush. Also, the two pairs were not as good as they first appeared because every other player had a pair of Jacks (from the flop). However, it was still a reasonable hand and they bet £10, although perhaps they should have checked.

2   Position 3 with their trips, plus the K ♦, Q ♦, J ♦, looked strong. But to press things this early on may have frightened off the others, so they decided to call the £10.

3   Position 5 was drawing to a double-ended straight (Queen, Jack, 10 and 9) and also had three consecutive hearts. This was a reasonable hand to continue with and so they called as well (£10).

4   Position 1 did have two pairs (Jacks and 4s), but because the Jacks were available to all, their feeling was that one of the other players would be holding better than a pair of 4s, and so would be beating them. However, they decided to stay in and called as well (a good example of loose play).

This equalised the pot, which now stood at £56.

The Turn

Round 1
The turn produced the 10 ♦, which helped both position 3 and position 5.

1   Position 2 saw no improvement in their hand and checked.

2   Position 3 welcomed the 10 ♦ because it gave them the chance of a royal flush, although the pretty strong three Jacks still remained as their hand. They now decided to go in stronger and bet £30.

3   Position 5 had seen their hand improve to two pairs (Jacks and 10s), with the possibility of a Queen-high straight. This is where poker becomes hard! Position 5 was reluctant to fold because they had two high pairs, plus the chance of a straight, but because the pair of Jacks were available to all, they did not feel confident. The recommendation in these situations is to fold if the pot has become expensive to stay in (which this one had) but on this occasion position 5 didn't do so and played on through calling.

4   Position 1 faced a similar tough decision. Their two pairs were of no real value, given everyone had Jacks anyway, but they did have the chance of a flush if a diamond appeared on the river. But later another player may have been in the same situation. Hence, position 1 folded (which was the correct course of action).

Round 2
1   Position 2, who had checked on the first round of betting after the flop, now decided to make the call (£30). At that point they held two pairs (Queens and Jacks) but if the river had brought an Ace, King, Queen, Jack or 10 they would have seen their hand improve in a number of ways (work out the combinations for yourself). This is probably why they stayed in, but – and this is open to debate –

perhaps they should not have done so, given that two of the Jacks were available to everyone.

The call from position 2 equalised the pot at a total £146.

The River

Round 1

1 Position 2 was the first to act. The 9 ♣ on the river did not do anything for them and they were still left with two pairs (Queens and Jacks). However, they went for a free look at what the others were going to do by checking.

2 The 9 ♣ gave player 3 a straight. But they decided to check as well, having pressed their bet in the last round.

3 Position 5 still felt pessimistic with their Jacks, 10s (the river did nothing for them either) but at least they could go through to the showdown for no extra cost. Hence, they checked.

The Showdown

Position 3 won the £146 pot with their straight. To win that pot they put in £54, so their profit was £92. All in all it was a pretty basic hand but interesting all the same. Player 2 would have been the most disappointed because any time a player has suited Ace and Queen as their hole-cards they are entitled to feel excited. What was also interesting about this hand was that the turn made the community cards look quite valuable. Yet, they were of no help to two of the players.

How the players felt about their hole-cards, and also how they felt as the community cards came along, is important to note because good poker players win money through being analytical rather than emotional. **But picture cards always make players feel excited.** Excitement is an emotion and thus there is always a need to step back from how the game is making you **feel**.

8

Winning Ways

F ollowing our analysis of some Texas Hold 'em hands, let's now look at some tips which will help newcomers increase their chances of winning at online poker.

Fixed-Limit Games

At this point it is worth noting that in our look at some winning ideas, we will continue to concentrate upon the fixed-limit version of Texas Hold 'em. Although most of the ideas will stand true for the other types of betting as well (pot-limit and no-limit), the strong recommendation is that newcomers stick with fixed-limit games. The pots can still build up quite nicely, but for newcomers there is little danger of losing all their money immediately – sadly a danger that very much exists with no-limit!

Stick to the Bankroll

A very strong recommendation is to set aside a bankroll to play with, generally around 300 times the big bet for the level of game you think you will be playing in. Hence, if the game is £2 / £4 have 300 times the £4 as your overall bankroll, which is a total of £1200. **Stick to this principle no matter how successfully your online poker career progresses.**

Keep Your Head

At the lower levels, fixed-limit games can be fast and furious with chips being thrown around almost like confetti. The tip here is to keep your head when all around you are losing theirs (with thanks to Rudyard Kipling!). Keep your head and maintain a policy of selective /aggressive play and you will have every chance of making money. Stick to the premium starting hands, plus possibly the occasional fling with something a bit less, but always bear in mind that you will probably still suffer more than the average number of bad beats due to the wildness of other players.

Position

- As we have seen, position is all important with Texas Hold 'em. Remember that your strategy should be to wait for the big hands, and then play them aggressively. But your position in the betting can often play a part in defining what are big hands and what are not. Supposing you are playing a game with nine other people. When you are in a late betting position, you may well consider, for example, a pair of 9s to be a bigger hand than when you are in an early one.

- Acting from an early position can often be harder than from a late one. However, in short-handed games (fewer than six players), while position is still important because the later a player is able to act the better, there is less chance of good hands being out there. In short-handed games you do not have to worry so much about the hands that could beat yours. Obviously, the better your hand, the more this will apply, but still remember how slightly weaker cards can be bet upon in short-handed games.

- It is not only your own position that you should be concerned with when playing Texas Hold 'em. Supposing a player that you have been able to mark down as a strong one (you'll know how to do this once you have read chapter 11 about note-taking) raises despite being 'under the gun'. What should be your action? Well, in the long run you will do better by assuming that the player making the raise holds at least the weakest of the hands which, as suggested in the tables in chapter 5, should be played from an early position. If you do not possess a hand that is of similar strength, the best thing to do will probably be to fold unless any notes you have taken indicate that the player making the raise is a 'bluffer', or you simply have a strong 'feeling' that this is the case.

- Another example of what the other players do relative to their positions can be illustrated through imagining you are holding a really strong pair of hole-cards. Supposing it is a pair of Aces and you are in a late betting position. Your normal reaction should be to make a raise, but if all of the players before you have already called, perhaps a call yourself might be the best option. You can then start to raise in later rounds (if there are any). The thinking here is that because a lot of players have called so early there might not be much strength in the hand. Therefore, an opening raise may frighten them all off. But once the game goes further and at least some of the players have bet more chips, they might then be reluctant to fold and will thus call a later raise.

- A further thing to note is that going into a flop alongside a lot of other players when you hold pocket Aces will mean a reduced chance of winning. Pocket Aces are great, but with five or six players going to the flop the likelihood is that someone will beat you unless the flop helps you out.
- On the other hand, in a late betting position it can sometimes be worthwhile playing on with a weaker pair, and then ditching them if the flop doesn't improve things, or if a lot of players don't fold on the next betting round. An example might be if you hold a pair of 4s. They are not very strong from an early position, but often worth calling with if in a late one (depending on how many players have stayed in). Then if the flop doesn't produce a third 4, which would yield a strong hand, you can fold. The odds against hitting trips on the flop are around 7 to 1. Therefore, if you believe that for every eight times you take this course of action you will be successful at least once, you may as well try it. The same policy can be adopted with suited connecting cards, such as 7, 8, or 10, Jack.
- Yet another crucial point about position and pairs is that the flop can easily ruin them. Let us imagine that you are in a game of ten players and seated in a late betting position. You are in possession of pocket Kings, but supposing six players go through to the flop with you? On the flop comes Ace, 10, 5. The Kings will not look quite so good now because out of the other 12 hole-cards still in play there is a reasonable chance of an Ace being present. If there is, the pair of Kings are second best. Remember, **regardless of the betting position**, the lower ranked the pair, the more chance the flop (or the turn or the river) will see them beaten. Of course, the flop could always help as well, which is why it is always worth at least considering going on to that point depending upon the strength of the pair and the cost associated with continuing.
- A final point about position is that if a player is in the dealer's seat they can sometimes attempt to 'steal' the blinds. Providing everyone has folded, a raise as the player's first action can sometimes force the two blinds to fold because they will be frightened off. If they don't fold, the player who made the raise can then always fold themselves if they feel their hand is not worth becoming involved with. Yes, it will mean some chips having been lost, but it is surprising how often blinds can be stolen in this way.

Calling

- A number of players are **bluffed out of a pot for the cost of just one more call**. Of course, one should only ever stay in when a hand offers at least a reasonable chance of winning anyway. This is because a player should not normally be progressing weak hands to the point where one more call will take them through to a showdown. Providing, though, a player does have a reasonable hand, they should try not to be forced out of a pot for the sake of one more call.
- Stick with calling bets on hands which can be drawn to, because in these instances a potential winning position will not yet have been established. Raising should be reserved for when a player has something substantial and wishes to attack, or for the rarer occasions when they want to try a bluff. Raising on the hope of drawing a strong hand is not usually a wise strategy.

Raising

- Remember that there are two main reasons for making a raise (there are more but these are the two most worthy of mention). First, a player will be trying to induce a fold from as many of their opponents as they can due to the fact that they have a weak hand and are purely bluffing. Second, a player will be trying to bring more money into the pot from any players that have not yet folded.
- Often players who hold strong hole-cards will raise despite being in very early betting positions. This sends out the message that they have a good hand, and also kicks off the possibility of a big pot. But it is equally important to remember that this is also a way of mounting a bluff. So, do not think that just because another player has made a very early raise they are particularly strong. Again, here is where any notes about your opponents will be a great help.

Check-Raise

Once a hand is in its late stages, a common method of trying to induce more betting from the other players is to check-raise. This can be a useful ploy when a player has a good hand and is through to the turn card. If everyone else has checked, anyone holding a strong hand should also consider doing so. This often leads another player to make a bet. Once it is the turn of the player who has the strong hand, they can then make a raise. Aside from possibly pulling more money into the pot, the situation may then exist where the other players feel they cannot walk away from how much they have invested so far – especially if they have a medium to strong hand. Hence, the raise might suck them in further.

Drawing to a Hand

- It will always be a good policy to steer well clear of low flush draws, like 4, 5, or 3, 4. Also, be very wary of chasing a straight when a flush is clearly possible. For example, if a player has 6, 7 non-suited with 4 ♣, 8 ♣, Ace ♥, K ♣ having come out on the flop and turn, there is a big chance someone else will already have a high flush (clubs), or will achieve it on the river. Yes, the player might still be able to achieve their straight, but a flush will beat them.
- A further point about drawing to a straight is that it is much better chasing the top end of one than the bottom. If K, 2 are the hole-cards and the flop produces 3, 4, 5 the temptation may be to carry on in the hope of hitting a 6 on the turn or the river. But in these instances don't forget that if a 6 does come out on the turn, anyone holding a 7 will have a higher hand. Then, on the river a 7 will be required just to tie.

Aces

Too many players make the error of sticking with their hole-cards just because one of them is an Ace. If you do have an Ace in the hole, only continue with it if the other card is higher than 8 or 9, although this rule can be relaxed a little if you are in the last couple of betting positions and plenty before you have folded. For example, going to the flop with Ace, 3 might seem like a good idea but even if another Ace comes out at that point, the low kicker will make your pair of Aces vulnerable.

Analyse the Board

- Whenever a player goes through to the flop, they should analyse the community cards with the aim of working out the best possible hand that might now be in play. It's a fairly simple task. Supposing the flop has produced two Aces along with a King, all non-suited. The best hand at that point would be four of a kind, that is if someone had pocket Aces.
- After the turn it will be possible to figure out a few hands which cannot be out there, and which cannot be created no matter what

cards come through on the river. An example would be if the flop and turn had produced 2 ♠, 8 ♥, Ace ♣, J ♦. In this case a flush is not going to be possible because the most of any one suit that can now be built into a hand is four (two hole-cards, one of the board cards, plus the still-to-come river card). The term used when the first four community cards are all of different suits is a 'rainbow board'.

- Note that the chances of a straight are greatly reduced when two cards of the same value come out on the flop.
- Once the river card has been dealt, there will be many more possible hands that can be eliminated. Work these out for yourself. However, even if you choose not to do so, at least remember that whenever you go through to the river it is absolutely essential to **analyse the board**. Once all the community cards have been dealt, it becomes very simple to work out the 'nut hand' (nut hand, or the 'nuts', is the poker term for the best hand that could be in play).
- If a player's hole-cards are a high pair, note they will be at a considerable advantage if a lower pair is dealt on the flop. Not only will they then have two pairs, they will also have the chance of a full house. Better still though, many of the other hands will have now been wrecked because of the pair on the board. For example, the chance of a straight will have been greatly reduced. Hence, in these situations a raise by the player holding the two pairs may well be an appropriate move.

Hot Streak

- Although there is absolutely no statistical evidence to back this up, most regular players will agree that this really does happen. Namely, that a number of 'hot' hands often appear to occur close together. For some reason of fate it seems that poker players, or any gamblers for that matter, rarely encounter regular patterns of winner, loser, winner, loser, etc. No, the general observation is that hot hands come in batches, followed by cold spells where hand after hand has to be folded.
- All that can be said about this is that all players, not just newcomers, have to be alert for when a hot streak takes place. However, it must not be a case of playing looser because you believe the cards will continue to run hot. Instead, a player who is enjoying a good run should be prepared to cut out of the game with their profits largely intact when the hot streak begins to cool. Players should never make the mistake of sitting there hoping the

hot run will come back. Eventually it might, but it will probably cost the player a good chunk of their profits while they are waiting for it to happen.

Pay Attention

This is critical. All players, especially newcomers, must try to never be surprised by what their hand has **become**. In long sessions this can be a problem because of tiredness. An example might be where a player has a pair of Jacks in the hole and the flop produces a third, along with 8, 5. The player would be delighted with their three Jacks and obviously go through to the turn. However, if the turn card produces an 8 they would have a full house – Jacks and 8s.

But after the turn they might not realise what they had and only call instead of possibly raise. The call would be based upon the strength of their three Jacks rather than their full house because they simply hadn't realised what they held. You may think this unlikely, but plenty of newcomers have had a similar experience. In this example it would stem from the player focusing so intently on their three Jacks that they fail to see beyond them.

Checking

- Even if a hand cannot be won, **never fold** if the option is there to check. After all, a check is a bet for nothing. There have been plenty of loose online games where players have been able to check through to the showdown for no cost. These instances have not resulted in many pots being won, but a few have been burgled! For example, it is certainly not unheard of for hands as low as a pair of 2s, 3s or 4s to take some reasonable pots. Indeed, in short-handed games, 'high-card' hands often scoop the cash.
- Always keep an eye open for players who fold when they could have checked. Chances are they will not know much about the mechanics of the game, or will be impatient for the hand to end and another to be dealt. Players like this are displaying signs of both ignorance and impatience, two traits that might mean they are fish!

Pull the Facts Together

Always pull all of the facts about a hand together. What does that mean? Simply, all players should analyse the board, analyse their hole-cards, analyse how many opponents are left in the hand, analyse how much is in the pot, and analyse their position in the betting. By pulling all these facts together, they'll be able to arrive at a better decision about whether to spend any further money on the hand. As an example, your pair of 9s might look interesting at first, but following the flop there's an Ace on the board, there are four other players left in, and your hand has not improved beyond the pair of 9s. Chances are that you are going to be beaten by someone, so save yourself the disappointment, not to mention the cash, and fold.

The Flop

For any hands that haven't already been folded, the flop should be the main point for dictating whether a player continues or not. Top poker players always say that the flop is the 'fit or fold' junction of a hand. If the flop does not help a player's hole-cards, they should always consider folding, no matter how good those hole-cards may have looked at first. The golden rule is **not to fall in love with your hole-cards**

The Turn

Although it can be a quiet betting point in a game, it is still the place where some players like to make a raise. This is because it can often be the cheapest place to do so. Think about it for a moment. After the turn card a lot of players might be waiting for the river to complete a hand. Therefore, if someone makes a raise at the turn other players may well still tread carefully. The advantage to someone who already holds a good hand is then twofold:

First, they can suck other players into the pot and thus increase their winnings if they do end up with the best hand.

Second, they can see how the other players react to the raise, and therefore possibly gain an insight into what those other players are holding.

Unless a player knows they have a really strong chance of winning, the river is not the ideal place to be entering into a raise, re-raise situation. After the river, another player might have drawn to an even better hand, but you may feel you have too good a hand to walk away from it. Therefore, it could become really expensive to see a showdown.

It is often better to draw the sting from others with a raise at the turn and then simply call at the river if another opponent looks strong. Alternatively, if a player is really confident, they could try the check-raise trap described earlier in this chapter.

The River

- After the river card has been dealt, all the players will be able to rule out there being four of a kind if at least two of the community cards are not the same rank. This is pretty obvious, but worth remembering if you happen to be holding a full house (four of a kind being one of only two hands that beats a full house).
- It is the same for a full house. If, after the river, two cards of the same rank are not on the board then a full house cannot be created. This will always be good news for any player sitting on a high flush. In a similar vein, if three cards of the same suit are not on the board after the river a flush cannot be out there.

Opponents

- Find players that you are better than, and then play at that level whenever possible. As a rule of thumb, the higher the stakes, the better the players. So, try to always play at a level where you are better than your opponents. Newcomers should only step up once they are confident they are better than those people who are already playing at the higher level.
- Of course, this will not be easy, because if a newcomer doesn't ever play at the higher level how can they improve? There is no easy answer here. It is a case of seeing how frequently you are winning on the lower-stakes tables before moving on only when you feel confident. But never forget that games can be observed without playing in them. This is often a good way to develop a feel for how a higher-level game is going.
- Newcomers should look out for the players who are determined to defend their blind bets (especially the big one) in a manner out of proportion to the cards they have received. Yes, to stay in the game can be less expensive from one of the blind positions, but that is no excuse for defending blinds regardless of how poor a set of hole-cards might be.
- But, some 'middling' hands which should not be played from any other position are worth pursuing from the big blind seat because the initial cost of doing so is less. Even then, though, many top players believe this should only be done if at least half of the table

has already folded. **Always remember that, unless a player is the only one left in, at the showdown only the best set of cards will win**.

- Play properly, and the looser the game, the more chance there is of winning. But what counterbalances this is that a high number of loose players will mean an increased amount of betting taking place. Hence, newcomers will soon notice that they might have to bet more when playing good hands. This obviously leads to higher pots, but there will be more financial exposure to bad beats because of the behaviour of their opponents.

- Another good rule of thumb for Texas Hold 'em is that a player should not invest in mediocre hands before their opponents reveal something about the strength of theirs. Naturally, though, newcomers in particular will need to hone their judgement about whether any strength that an opponent shows is genuine or just a bluff.

Still on the topic of opponents, to end this chapter let's briefly examine the different types of online Texas Hold 'em player that newcomers will encounter. Over the years they have all been given nicknames. You will see why from the write-ups of each one!

It is very important for a newcomer to know about the different types of player because if you happen to learn that a game consists solely of 'Mad Hatters' the advice would be to buy in double quick. Alternatively, if you come to realise that a game is full of 'Professors', gather up your chips and scoot.

'The Rock' aka Passive, Tight or Pro

This type of player becomes involved in very few hands, preferring to sit tight and wait for the exceptional opportunities. An individual like this will generally play Aces and Kings from the hole, but little else. Furthermore, they are very good at knowing when they are beaten on pocket Aces. When 'The Rock' is dealt good hole-cards, they also know exactly how to play them. Being a good reader of the game (very good at analysing the community cards), they rarely run the risk of unexpected big losses. This is definitely a player to be very wary of, although perhaps you might be able to pull off a bluff or two on them, as they will simply not be drawn into playing poor hole-cards.

'The Mad Hatter' aka Loose, Casual, Loudmouth or Aggressive

Almost the complete opposite of 'The Rock', this type of player is exactly who you want to meet. Full of bravado, they play really loosely, or simply don't know how to play at all (but think they do!). Late Friday evenings can see a lot of these players logging into the bigger sites. This is because the pubs have closed and, egged on by alcohol and their mates, 'The Mad Hatters' will be throwing their chips around and boasting to all and sundry via the chat box just how macho they are. Let this type of player carry on deluding themselves while you quietly take their chips.

'The Grinder' aka Loose or Einstein

This is a player who tends to play at set times every few days, most probably at weekends. They like the fun of playing and hope to win, but they don't have any major talent. However, they have picked up some bits and pieces about the way to play and can be a problem when the run of the cards goes with them. Overall, they will be hoping to grind out a little profit from something they regard primarily as relaxation. But, although you should keep a close eye on them if they start winning a few pots, it should not be that difficult to separate them from their chips.

'The Professor' aka The Man, Tight, Aggressive or Pro

This is the player to avoid at all costs, even in front of 'The Rock'. This is the type of individual which other top players regard as having written the book on the online game, not to mention actually playing to it! 'The Professor' can't be bluffed because they will spot a bluff a mile off and will also play aggressively when their cards are right. The best thing here is not to stay in any game where another player starts to look like a 'Professor'.

'Calling Station' aka Loose or Passive

These are almost certainly fish, and exactly the kind of player newcomers should be looking for. Players like these simply stay in pot after pot, regardless of how little chance they have of winning. They then end up calling at the showdown because they eventually realise that their opponents are not going to go away. Needless to say, they inevitably lose, but they continually fail to appreciate how this is happening because of their obsession with staying in hands no matter how poor their cards are. Look out for 'Calling Station' players and you will not go far wrong.

'The Student' aka Hibernator, Tight or Einstein

A player who almost always goes by the book, 'The Student' takes very few chances, but as yet lacks the ability of 'The Professor' to throw the book away and smash into a hand just to upset the thinking of their opponents. Inexperienced and rigid in their play, they also have to be careful about going bust as they have a limited bankroll. In the right circumstances they are an opponent to look out for, because in a heads-up (playing against a single opponent) they will probably crumble in the face of an aggressive betting attack.

'The Pretender' aka Chameleon, Aggressive or Loudmouth

This is someone to be extremely wary of. This kind of player will try to give the impression they are a 'Mad Hatter' in order to suck their opponents in. But the little bit of stake money they will spend in doing so is really an investment. Why? Simply because 'The Pretender' will be a player who knows a lot about the game and is extremely adept at reading the other players. 'The Pretender' will check, raise and call in seemingly illogical order, but will then take the pot with poor cards after everyone else has folded for fear of what they are holding. Play with opponents like this at your own risk!

'The Texan Terror' aka Loudmouth, Loose, Casual or Intoxicated

Often a player with a huge bankroll, this is the kind of opponent who will use the chat box to bitch about the game, the online site, the cards and their opponents. When they win they can't resist boasting, but when they lose they don't care because they have a lot of money to begin with. This is definitely the kind of player to look out for because they can be relieved of their chips without too much fuss, especially at pub closing time on Friday or Saturday nights!

'Miss Mystery' aka Chameleon, Pro or Hibernator

This is the kind of player who deliberately tries to disguise their real ability. They are not as obvious about it as 'The Pretender', but their intention is the same: to suck their opponents in and then take their chips. This kind of player will make the occasional stupid comment in the chat box and will call weak hands all the way to the river before revealing their losing cards. But afterwards if you reviewed the hands they did this on you'd find they were the ones that were for small pots. However, 'Miss Mystery' will play a much tighter game when it matters! They are known as 'Miss' because they will often appear to play, dare it be said, 'like a girl'. They are generally players, though, that keep their head down waiting for the right opportunity. Be careful around them.

9

Managing Your Money and Managing Your Mood

No matter what they are betting upon, far too many gamblers do not pay enough attention to the topic of money management. One reason for this might be that the whole idea of managing stake money appears dull compared to the betting action. On the other hand, it could be that many gamblers lack self-control, or simply that they are very good at deluding themselves. Whatever it is, any punter that fails to employ at least some form of money management is going to fail.

Incidentally, self-delusion is a bit of a problem with punters. The number of times gamblers say they 'break even', or might have finished a 'bit in front', never fails to surprise. The truth is that most punters lose, some worse than others – but they still lose. With online poker, many players manage to win their fair share of hands, but they still end up losing overall. Therefore the conclusion can only be that punters are losing more than they need to simply because they are failing to manage their stake money properly. Given the speed with which online poker is played, managing stakes is crucially important.

Staking Money (Bankroll)

Once a newcomer is at the point they are ready to buy into a game, they will have already deposited money with the online poker site. The amount deposited is up to each individual but the absolute golden rule is that **nobody should ever gamble more money than they can afford to lose.**

Fortunately, most people are sensible and so it is good advice to deposit an amount of cash that is in proportion to the staking level of the games that are going to be played in. Naturally, the higher the stakes, the more money will need to be made available.

As the very first step in managing their bankroll, players can either make a sum of money available for only the session they intend to play in, or allocate an amount for a much longer period. The recommendation is to do the latter because the amount deposited in this way can be more easily thought of as set to one side for poker playing.

Also, by playing in a selective / aggressive way, a player will be able to take advantage of when the cards come good for them. Therefore, if they have allocated enough stakes for a decent period of time they will be able to weather the sessions when the hands fail to materialise and they end up losing. The latter occasionally happens to even the best players, not least because the blind bets eventually eat away at even the biggest pile of chips.

So, how much should a player allocate for, say, three months' worth of online play?

A good idea is to set aside an amount which is 300 times the maximum bet of the typical game which an individual will be playing in. Hence, in a £1 / £2 game a player should kick off with a bankroll of 300 times the £2, which is £600.

To make this easier, the following table can be used as a quick-reference guide. It shows the amount a newcomer should consider putting aside as a bare minimum for the different levels of games they might play in. It also shows the recommended amount which many experts believe a newcomer should embark upon their poker-playing career with. Finally, it illustrates the amount which should be accumulated before any player moves up to the games with the next highest level of stakes ('move up amount').

Game Level	Bare Minimum	Recommended	Move up Amount
£0.50 / £1	£100	£300	£600
£1 / £2	£200	£600	£1200
£2 / £4	£400	£1200	£1800
£3 / £6	£600	£1800	£3000
£5 / £10	£1000	£3000	£4800
£10 / £20	£2000	£6000	£9000
£20 / £40	£4000	£12,000	£18,000

Let's briefly discuss this move up amount. Over the short time that online poker has been in existence, many players have accumulated a bankroll which has allowed them to move up to higher-staking games. But many of these players have then started to lose because their skills were not sharp enough to compete with the better players, or perhaps because they simply hit a bad run of cards.

Therefore, the recommendation is that if a player sees their bankroll dip below the move up amount they should return to the game at the next lowest staking level. At first this will mean dipping in and out of the higher-level games until their bankroll stabilises above the move up amount, but this is better than seeing all of it quickly destroyed at the higher levels.

A final point about a newcomer's overall bankroll is that they should probably refrain from keeping it all at one poker site. The big operators are extremely unlikely to go bust, but if anyone chooses to play on a fledgling site the recommendation is that they only ever move small amounts of cash into it. Thus, if the site does happen to go under (it has happened on a few rare occasions) they will not suffer too much pain.

Buying In

With online poker, money management is not only about controlling stakes. Sometimes it is also about using the stakes to gain an advantage over the other players. This begins when a player first buys into a game.

The feeling among seasoned poker players is that a new player should always enter a game with as big a pile of chips as possible. A rule of thumb is to work out what the typical buy-in is for a table and then go to the table with twice that amount if possible. This is a carry-over from real-life games.

With real-life games, players often like to appear high-rollers from the start. Their feeling is that this might put them at a psychological advantage over their opponents. But in many ways this thinking is flawed. Real-life games tend to see the players stay in for long periods. Hence, if a game has been running for five hours a player with a big pile of chips may not have actually won them; they may still be sitting on them from when they first bought in. Observant opponents will always remember when a player bought in big and so once that player has taken part in a few hands any perceived advantage they thought their buy-in gave them might well be lost.

However, with internet poker things are different. Online games see players come and go with great frequency. Thus, if you enter a game and see that another player has a large pile of chips you will have no idea whether that player has been winning, losing, or has simply stayed even.

As an example, if you enter a £3 / £6 game where the typical buy-in is £200 it can be an advantage to bring £400 to the table. Anyone who comes into the game after you, providing you have not quickly lost a large chunk of your chips, will tend to think you have managed to double your buy-in rather than having entered the game with it in the first place. You may laugh at this, but it's a constant surprise how naive many online poker players are. That naivety will often lead to players giving more respect than is necessary to someone with a big pile of chips. The result is that the player with the bigger pile of chips can sometimes pull off bluffs with relatively poor cards.

But let's sound a note of caution here. Buying in big does not mean that you need to play big all the time. Selective / aggressive is still the key, and the core of that strategy is to sit tight and mostly play only good hands. Try to pull off the occasional bluff, or perhaps **sometimes** play weaker hole-cards from late betting positions, but sitting patiently and playing the waiting game will make newcomers money in the long run.

Of course, there is also a very practical reason for buying in big. Once you are in a game, many sites place restrictions on how much you can re-buy into a game with after losing all of your chips. Therefore, it is better to make sure you have enough in front of you to play for the length of time you have allocated, rather than be disappointed later on.

Posting

When first entering a game, players can either sit waiting for the blinds to reach them, or they can post a blind straight away. Taking the former course of action means they will not be included in the deal until the big blind has reached them. Taking the latter course means they will be included in the very next deal. So, if you enter a game and the blinds are not far away, the advice is not to post. Instead, simply wait the short time before the blinds come around and then start playing.

Naturally, it could be that a player enters a game just after the blinds have passed by their position. In this case the player may wish to post a blind in order to become involved in the action as soon as possible. However, the best course of action again is to wait for the blinds to come around, using the time to observe the other players and possibly picking up some clues about the way they are playing.

As a matter of interest, once in a game, keep an eye open for what newcomers do when they enter the fray. There could be an online tell here. **Should a new player post the big blind despite the blinds being about to reach them, they might be a loose player who is simply unable to wait before throwing some chips around like confetti!**

To Quit or Not to Quit?

This is another topic that causes a great deal of debate between poker experts. One school of thought is that once you have won or lost a predetermined amount you should pack up for the day. However, a rival point of view is that you should play until the point comes where you either have to, or want to, stop.

Although the first argument is marginally more sensible, the second is worth examining as well. This particular viewpoint is based upon the thinking that it makes no difference when you play. The saying among some poker players is '**The next hour you play is the next hour you play**'. In other words, if you win a predetermined amount, unless you are going to quit playing poker forever, it is all one long game anyway.

Because there is merit in each argument, what follows are the good and bad points for each of them. In the end, though, it is still up to the individual to decide what they want to do.

Quitting a Game After a Predetermined Sum Has Been Won or Lost

The Good:

✔ Nobody will win hand after hand. Therefore, if a player reaches their predetermined profit figure they should not try to buck the trend. Quitting and coming back refreshed for the next session is the best thing to do.

✔ If a player has a bad run, they must not allow it to spoil the next time they play due to losing more than they are comfortable with in a single session. So, after a player has lost a predetermined amount it is best to stop and then come back next time in a more positive frame of mind.

✔ Once a player has won a predetermined amount, they should quit the game and enjoy their profits. Winning, for example £200 in one hour, is the same as winning £200 in eight hours, except for the seven extra hours spent online! If £200 is the desired profit figure, and it is achieved in one hour, then there will be plenty of time for other things, like paying some attention to the wife or doing the gardening!

✔ Any players that quit when they have lost a predetermined amount might actually be taking themselves out of games they had no right to be in anyway. The overall policy should be that if any player ever finds they are in a game where the other players are much better, they should leave as soon as possible. Trouble is, in the heat of a losing battle, players sometimes do not appreciate how they are being outclassed. Therefore, if they have a policy of quitting after having lost a predetermined amount they could be saving themselves from an even worse result.

The Bad:
✗ Through quitting once they are a certain amount of money in front, players might be preventing themselves from winning even more.
✗ Through stopping after a predetermined amount has been lost, there is no chance to win back some of that loss.
✗ Depending upon what level it is set at, players might rarely reach their predetermined profit or loss amount, and so will end up playing until they either have to, or want to, stop anyway.
✗ On the other hand, through having strict predetermined profit or loss figures, players may end up not playing very much – simply because they keep hitting their targets quickly (not that this would be bad in the case of profits!).

Quitting a Game Only When a Player Either Has To, or Wishes To, Stop

The Good:
✔ When a player is hot, they will be able to take full advantage. If they are in the right game and are winning money, why not milk it for as much as possible?
✔ Playing for as long as practical is going to allow a player to build up a greater level of experience, and also possibly offer that player more of an opportunity to construct notes about their opponents.
✔ Playing on and winning more will do wonders for a player's confidence, not to mention their bankroll.

The Bad:
✗ If a player encounters a losing spell, it could be badly exacerbated through continuing to play.
✗ Continuing to play when things are going wrong could badly affect a player's confidence, corrupting their judgement for another day.
✗ A player could end up sitting in front of their PC for extremely long periods, possibly to the detriment of other things in their life.

So, that's a brief look at the arguments for whether players should quit when they hit a predetermined profit or loss figure, or if they should just play until they have to, or wish to, stop.

But there is another way of looking at it. Some players employ the strategy of setting a limit on the number of maximum bets they will make. So, if the game is £10 / £20 they might stop after they have made, for example, 25 maximum bets. This will be regardless of whether they are winning or losing. It seems a reasonable thing to do, but anybody employing this strategy will still be left with the problem of it possibly being a long time before they hit their pre-set limit of maximum bets. All in all then, it is far from clear what to do for the best!

However, bearing in mind that people have different ideas over this, here is one suggestion with regard to the best way to play:

Set a maximum amount of money that you are prepared to win or lose in each session. Then, if that amount is reached, stop playing. But also set a time limit for your play after which you will stop regardless of whether you are making a profit or a loss. Providing you set a time limit that is reasonable compared to what is going on in the rest of your life, you will therefore never be left sitting in front of your PC for hours on end vainly trying for a profit figure that you are unable to reach, or trying to recover from a loss that you did not want to make in the first place.

Keeping Track

Regardless of whether, or how, players choose to limit their online poker sessions, it is essential they keep a record of their financial progress. This is the thing that most punters find very difficult to do. Unfortunately, most punters only tend to remember their last win! What separates the winning gamblers from the losing ones is the ability to be realistic and keep records.

Serious punters, online poker players being no exception, should treat their gambling as a business. No business can survive without records, so it follows that no serious online poker player can do so either.

There are a number of advantages in keeping accurate and honest records. But to be of any use, the records will need to reflect two things:

- The 'win rate' – the average amount of cash won or lost per hour spent playing.
- The 'standard deviation' figure – this will measure short-term fluctuations.

Together these two things will quickly determine a player's average hourly 'expectation'. To determine this figure, the following will need to be done:

- Record the buy-in figure for every session.
- Show the game limits.
- Write down the amount of cash won or lost at the end of each hour (or part of it). These figures will be required to work out the standard deviation (more about that shortly).
- Upon leaving the game, record the amount of profit or loss made and the number of hours played.

Discovering an hourly win or loss rate is quite simple. All that needs to be done is divide the amount of money won or lost by the number of hours played. Thus, if someone has played for four hours and won £100 their win rate would be £25 per hour. On the other hand, a deficit of £60 over a four-hour session would equate to a loss rate of £15 per hour.

Simple so far, but will whatever figure arrived at be an accurate reflection of the play? It might not be, due to how a player may have staked much more in one hour than they did in another. So, what players really need to discover is how much risk they took with their bankroll in order to achieve the profit or loss figure.

An example might be that two players each show an hourly profit figure of £20. However, one of these players may have seen very little swing in their stake money – say, never more than £100 up or £100 down – while the other might show the opposite. This second player may have seen big swings in their bankroll, sometimes being £400 down and sometimes £600 up. The fluctuation experienced in achieving the same profit figure is known as variance.

It is important to measure variance because the less variance shown in reaching any given profit figure, the smaller the risk that was taken with the bankroll. Clearly, this is going to be a big factor in deciding how well a player has been performing. Unfortunately, arriving at a variance figure takes a little more work than simply calculating an hourly win or loss rate.

Standard Deviation

You are going to love this bit! The way of measuring variance is to find the standard deviation. Don't be alarmed though; this book is not developing into a lesson on statistics. That said, keen mental arithmetic skills will serve anyone well when playing poker. Hence, a bit of statistical work now will not come amiss! If you are not a fan of statistics, console yourself through considering that the lower your standard variation, the lower your bankroll will need to be in order to withstand the peaks and troughs experienced during every game.

Measuring standard deviation looks harder than it actually is. Supposing a player has played for five hours and each hour has seen them win or lose a different amount.

Hour	Money Won or Lost	Deviation
1	Won £30	− £1
2	Won £60	+ £29
3	Lost £40	+ £9
4	Lost £10	− £21
5	Won £15	− £16

1 Over the five hours' play their profit was £55 (£30 + £60 − £40 − £10 + £15). Divide that £55 by five to arrive at an hourly win rate of £11.

2 To find the deviation figure, first add up the 'Money Won or Lost' figures, ignoring whether they were actually profit or loss, and then divide this by the number of hours played. Hence, £30 + £60 + £40 + £10 + £15 equals £155. Divide £155 by 5 to arrive at £31.

3 The deviation figure (the one in the last column of the table) is found through comparing the £31 against the actual Money Won or Lost figure for each hour. It still does not matter whether the money was actually won or lost; all that counts is how the figures compare to the £31. **(A good way of telling if you have got this right is if all the figures in the deviation column total up to zero. This is because the positive variations will always cancel out the negative ones.)**

4 However, we cannot simply work out an average of the deviation figures, because some were positive and some were negative. This is overcome through squaring (multiplying a number by itself) each deviation. The reason each number is squared is because multiplying a negative by a negative will always produce a positive.

5   Therefore, the table now looks like this:

Hour	Money Won or Lost	Deviation
1	Won £30	−£1 x −£1 = **£1**
2	Won £60	+£29 x +£29 = **£841**
3	Lost £40	+£9 x +£9 = **£81**
4	Lost £10	−£21 x −£21 = **£441**
5	Won £15	−£16 x −£16 = **£256**

6   Add up the new deviation figures (in bold) to arrive at £1620. Divide that by 5 (5 hours played) and the sum is **£324**. This is the **variance**.

7   Lastly, because this variance figure is a squared value, you now need to discover the square root of it in order to keep it in the same proportion as the figures drawn from the game. In other words, nothing else was squared so the variance figure cannot be either. Thus, the square root of £324 is £18. This is known as the **standard deviation**.

Once you begin playing, continually calculate your standard deviation figure. Although it looks a long-winded thing to do, it is an excellent way for players to compare the amount of risk they took in each game. Each time a player's standard deviation is lower than it was for a previous session they will know that they risked less money in achieving whatever result they came away from the game with (profit or loss). The opposite will be the case if it is higher. But if you don't fancy this kind of arithmetic, help is at hand anyway.

Simply search the internet for 'poker software'. As you might expect, there is plenty out there and some of it has been designed to help players measure their hour-by-hour, day-by-day, week-by-week, etc. performance, including standard deviation and average hourly win/loss rates.

However, regardless of whatever method players choose to record their standard deviation, they should all have the same objective, namely, **minimising their standard deviation while maximising their winnings.**

This means putting as little of their stake at risk as possible while still winning as much as possible. Of course, this is much easier to say than to do. The greater the number of bets made, the higher the standard deviation. But this takes us back to selective / aggressiveness.

Any player who plays the right cards in the correct way will almost certainly not be risking as much of their bankroll as a player who takes part in lots of hands.

Risk

Another interesting thing to note about standard deviation is how it can help measure a player's attitude to risk. The higher the standard deviation figure, the more risk has been taken. Whether that risk was worth it can only be measured against how much the player won or lost in the session. Obviously, a high standard deviation figure coupled with a loss is not good news. But while a profit is the aim, if the profit was a low one compared to the standard deviation figure, the question should be whether it was worth the risk.

Put simply, if a player is not happy with a high level of risk they should look to keep their standard deviation low. The same applies if they are playing with only a small bankroll.

Something to note here, though, is that the looser the game that is played in, the harder it will be to maintain a low standard deviation figure. This will be due to the fact that, in loose games, the players throw money around considerably more. Therefore, to stay in the pots where they have good cards will probably cost players more. Yes, they will win bigger pots but it will still mean their standard deviation figure being higher.

Profit or Loss

We have now looked at a number of topics to do with managing your money, but we have left the most straightforward one to last. Through doing so it will hopefully have the most impact. Quite simply, if a player does nothing else to manage their bankroll, they must at least keep track of whether they are winning or losing at online poker.

No matter what is being bet upon, any gambler that fails to keep a financial record of their bets is doomed to failure.

Paperwork

By now it is probably pretty obvious that to be a successful online poker player there is a requirement to manage your bankroll in some form or another. But whatever degree this is taken to there will be a need to carry out at least some paperwork. Using a PC it should not take long, but the key to making it work will be to keep it up. It is no good doing it for a couple of months and letting it lapse. No, it must be kept up to date and then reviewed regularly. The top online players do it despite the perceived image of a 'card sharp' gambler not necessarily suggesting this would be the case, so it should be the same for newcomers.

Mood Management

Your mood can make or break, especially break, any amount of disciplined and analytical online poker play (don't laugh, you'll be surprised). It is important to introduce this topic here because after analysing some hands, looking at winning techniques, and discussing money management you'll probably be raring to go. It's good stuff if you are, but first be aware, in fact be very aware!

Earlier on in this book the point was made that the best way to win money online is to find players that you know you can beat. In other words, play against fish. Of course, you will start off as a fish yourself (although not such a tiddler as others because you will have read this book). But even once you have learned to swim, it is still important that you don't be gobbled up by the bigger fish. Sadly, with online poker this is an easy thing to have happen – that is, unless you manage your mood.

Screaming in Cyberspace

Playing poker online is a pretty lonely occupation. Yes, there are going to be chat boxes where you can communicate with the other players, but they are no real substitute for sitting at a table surrounded by human beings.

The value of having other human beings playing the game near you should not be underestimated. It's not about when you are winning; it's about when you are losing. No matter what they are betting upon, all punters will lose sometimes. Indeed, most punters lose more often than they win. However, if the amount of money won outweighs the amount lost this will not matter. Sadly, this is rarely the case. This is a shame because most punters do tend to win their fair share of hands when playing online poker.

What spoils things for many, though, is that when they lose they lose so badly. In other words, they tend to go 'on tilt'. The unfortunate thing about this is that a short spell on tilt can absolutely ruin weeks – or even months – of careful and profitable punting, no matter whether that punting has been with the horses, dogs or online poker. So, it seems pretty clear that any gambler who can successfully control their moods (their emotions) when they hit a bad spell is going to be a winner.

To some extent the same applies when punters hit a winning streak, although, by their nature, winning streaks are obviously not as destructive as losing ones can be. That said, any punter who allows their mood to overtake rational thought when they are winning might well ultimately fail to take advantage of their hot spell.

So, a big part of gambling with online poker is about mood management because most of the time you will be playing alone.

Bad beats are the things to be most aware of. A 'bad beat' is the slang term for when a poker player loses a hand they would usually expect to win. For example, it might be that you and one other player have gone through to the turn card. You are sitting on three Aces and through some aggressive, but nevertheless controlled, betting have seen a decent pot build up. Your remaining opponent has already shown that they are a loose player and are very short on chips. Thus you are confident of taking the pot.

Your opponent is first to act. They go all-in. This doesn't worry you because of how they have been playing, and also because you have such a good hand. Therefore you call. The cards are exposed ready for the river.

However, when the river card is dealt you are horrified to see that it gives your opponent a really low straight, a straight finished off only by both the turn and river cards. What is more, the straight was built upon two hole-cards spaced three cards apart. In other words, they went through to the end needing the flop, the turn and the river cards to help them out. This is known as taking a bad beat – what is more, a bad beat at the hands of a player who did little right.

In a real-life game your consequent frustration can quite easily be taken out on others. You can curse the dealer or the other player (and then apologise). You can throw your cards back to the dealer (and then apologise), or you can simply ask for sympathy from the rest of the table. But whatever you do you will have vented your spleen quickly and then, certainly in the first two instances, had to overcome your annoyance because of the need to apologise. However, as the saying goes, in cyberspace nobody can hear you scream.

Sitting alone at your PC, you can do very little to express your anger at the bad beat. Yes, you can shout or hurl one of your possessions across the room, but the speed of internet poker will have already led to another hand being dealt. These are the times when there is a huge danger of your frustration being expressed through a series of poor decisions, wrong-sized bets, or perhaps even both. This can easily wreck hours of careful and disciplined selective / aggressive play, and at the same time give back a sizeable chunk of your hard-earned chips.

So, do not allow a bad beat to ruin the next few hands for you. If you do suffer a really bad stroke of luck, quickly click the sit-out button and regain your composure. At the moment you might laugh at this, believing that you will always be able to keep your self-control. Perhaps you are one of those special people who will, but you'll be a rare human being if you can! There are very few serious online poker players who have not reacted to a bad beat in a way they then quickly regretted. So, save yourself the drama – manage your mood; and if need be, click that sit-out button.

Just This Once

Another mood to control when playing online poker is 'just this once'. If you don't, it can be costly. It is most likely to overtake you after a long series of poor hole-cards. For example: you are in a late betting position and have been dealt yet another bad hand, say 9, 3 non-suited. Before it is your turn to act, three other players fold and of the remainder nobody raises. Starved of action, you suddenly convince yourself that the community cards are bound to improve your hand, so you think 'just this once' and click the call button. As soon as doing so you regret it and then end up watching the flop with a crazed interest. Of course, the flop does nothing for your 9, 3 and you regain your senses enough to fold. But it was still a wasted bet.

The really sad thing about 'just this once' is that it can also lead to players pressing on with poor hands when the flop does not help them. Using our example of having 9, 3 non-suited, supposing the flop brings another 3. You have now got a low pair. Normally you wouldn't play it, but because you have already made a rash bet you might feel the need to defend it. Thus, you are further sucked in. Occasionally, this way of playing will reap dividends, but definitely not as many times as it will lead to disappointment. Hence, be extremely wary of falling into a 'just this once' mood.

Just One More

'Just one more' is probably even more dangerous than 'just this once' and is a way of thinking, or mood, which many gamblers find themselves in without ever realising it. A few years ago a punter in a betting shop could be saved from this because the shop had to close at the end of the day. And even though modern times have brought the advent of extended shop hours with all kinds of things for the punters to bet upon, the shops still eventually have to close. Internet poker, though, never shuts down. Games can be played 24 hours a day, 7 days a week. The result is that online poker players need to rely upon their own discipline not to fall into the trap of 'just one more'.

So, what is a 'just one more' mood? It is when a player carries on playing despite having set themselves a clear set of rules for when they intended to stop. It might be they have said they will play for two hours and then pack up, or perhaps play only up to a certain time. Alternatively, they may have set themselves profit or loss figures that if arrived at will be the point at which they intend to stop playing. But whatever they have decided to use as a way of limiting their play, it can be extremely easy to fall into a 'just one more' mood. All experienced online poker players will confirm this because they have all done it.

Quite honestly, 'just one more' tends to be more a problem of not being able to stop playing rather than not being able to stop gambling. The issue is that the former can't be separated from the latter. Because the playing can't be split from the **gambling**, it is all too easy to lose profits, or increase losses, through playing just one more hand, then one more after that, etc.

Therefore, please be very aware of falling into this kind of mood. If need be, write yourself a note and stick it to your PC, reminding yourself of the dangers associated with 'just one more'. But in the end you will still need to show enough discipline to actually stop playing at, or very close to, whatever limits you have set yourself for your online poker session.

A Virtual Chip on Your Shoulder

One of the most famous poker films of all time is *The Cincinnati Kid*. A noticeable feature, if rather minor, about the poker action in this film is that it takes place with cash. Every game sees various denominations of dollar bills being counted out and then bet, won, lost, or just generally handled by the players. Watch it next time it is broadcast and you'll soon come to enjoy the delicious sound of the money as it rustles its way through everyone's hands!

In games where cash is the betting medium, it is easy to keep a perspective on how much you are winning or losing. However, when chips are used in real-life games some of that perspective is lost. Under pressure, players can start to divorce the chips from the money it took to buy them. The feel and the sound of the chips can be quite powerful, inducing in a player the desire to assemble more of them; but in the end they are not money. Sadly, though, with internet games the gap between paper money and the virtual chips is even wider.

Playing online you do not have the opportunity to handle your chips, let alone cash. On the internet, chips are just a virtual commodity. Because there are neither chips nor money in front of you, it is easy to lose sight of how much you are winning or losing. In fact, one or two well-known successful online poker players keep a couple of well-worn casino chips with them as they play. Through frequently picking one of the chips up and deftly turning it through their fingers (something they first started to do while learning their trade in many an all-night poker session), they are adamant they can maintain their focus over how the virtual chips translate to money.

Of course, many poker experts believe that the key to being a good player is having the ability to divorce the chips from the money. They put forward the view that the more a player thinks about the cash they are playing with, the less inclined they will be to play big when the need arises. But for a newcomer that could be a dangerous thing to do. No, there is a crucial need to remember the link between those virtual chips and the cash it took to buy them. Should the connection in your mind between the chips and the cash ever begin to blur, why not sit out a couple of hands and go and get your wallet? Open it and feel the cash within (hopefully, you will have some!) and then think about how much you bought into the game for. Through doing this, you'll soon restore your respect for those virtual chips. If this doesn't happen, stop playing immediately!

That last point was a slightly light-hearted suggestion about how not to end up with a virtual chip on your shoulder, but please never overlook the importance of mood management. For all the pleasure, not to mention profit, it can bring, online poker is one of the most addictive things now available to gamblers. Anyone who approaches it without being aware of how it could easily grip them is going to struggle to avoid a heavy loss, let alone make a profit.

Bluffing and Online Tells

Bluffing and online tells are two topics which make sense to examine together, as in many ways they are related. This is because a good bluff is one of the ways an online tell can be induced from an opponent.

Bluffing

When online poker first began, many seasoned real-life players shunned it because they believed **bluffing** was not going to play a large enough part. Perhaps they were correct, but a bluff is a bluff no matter how the game is being played, although it must be said that a good bluffer will be able to use that strength more in a real-life game than they will with the online version.

Players use bluffs to mislead opponents over the value of their hands. Usually they are executed in one of two basic ways and for fairly obvious reasons.

1 Players bet heavily to deceive opponents into thinking that they are in possession of a stronger hand than they actually are. This is done to try to force their opponents into folding, rather than have them call, bet or raise and perhaps go through to the showdown. Executing a bluff in this way can lead to winning a pot with the poorest set of cards at the table.

2 Early in a hand, players bet lightly in order to disguise the strength of the cards they hold. The objective of this type of bluff is to try to keep as many opponents in the pot as possible. Yes, those opponents will be spending less when they call but this should be offset by keeping more of them in the game for longer, thus making the pot bigger at the end.

Both points should demonstrate that bluffing can be carried out just as much in internet games as it can in real-life ones. Therefore, why do so many seasoned poker players feel bluffing is of no value online? The answer is because online games do not allow experienced poker players to be able to 'read' their opponents. For example, the internet version of the game is clearly not going to allow one player to see if, for example, a nerve in the neck of an opponent starts to twitch when they come under pressure (as is far from uncommon in real-life games). But there is plenty of compensation for this because there are most definitely a number of online tells. They cannot be ignored and so we will look at them shortly. First, though, let's look at an example of an actual bluff being executed in a Texas Hold 'em game.

Texas Hold 'em is a game where bluffing sometimes has to be used, regardless of whether the game is a real-life one or on the internet. The reason is that the small and big blinds required every hand will soon eat up even the largest pile of chips unless it is at least occasionally supplemented through winning some pots. So, any player who is low on chips and suffering a bad run of cards may well have to play a few bluffs. (In tournament play this becomes even more essential because once a player's chips have been lost they are eliminated. The only exception to this is if the tournament is still in its re-buy period.)

It is important to remember that when a player has a low stack of chips they will quickly become vulnerable. As a result their opponents may well start to bluff them out of pots. They will attempt this knowing that any player with a small pile of chips is going to be reluctant to chance them on inferior hands. Hence, a player in this position is going to have to pull off some bluffs of their own, or risk being wiped out.

So, let's look at a bluff in action.

Five players at the table. The game is £20 / £40 with small blinds of £15 and big blinds of £30. It's big-time stuff with the minimum bet or raise being £60. In the first round the maximum bet or raise is £200, but after the flop it is £400.

Hole-cards

(We join the game with the betting about to begin.)

Deal 1

Position 1 (dealer)	Position 2 (small blind)	Position 3 (big blind)	Position 4

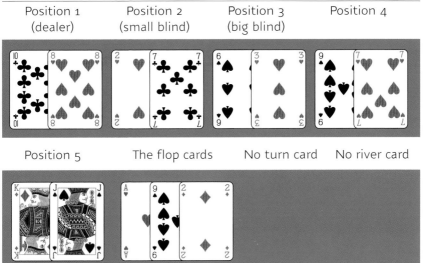

Position 5	The flop cards	No turn card	No river card

Betting Round 1

1   Position 2 puts in the small blind.

2   Position 3, who has a low stack of chips due to a recent bad run, puts in the big blind.

3   Position 4 folds.

4   Position 5, who is doing reasonably well and likes the look of his King and Jack, raises by putting in £200.

5   Position 1 folds.

Betting Round 2

1   Position 2 folds.

2   Position 3 is in trouble. With a very low stack of chips they do not have enough stakes to keep covering many more blinds. They have no hand but decide to go for a big bluff, given that only player 5 remains in. Hence, they call the £200 (meaning they have to stake £170 because they have already bet the £30 big blind).

The pot is therefore equalised at a total of £415.

The Flop
Betting Round 1

1   Position 3 is the first to act and they decide they want to continue with their bluff despite the flop doing little for them (there is the chance of an Ace, 2, 3, 4, 5 straight if the right cards come out on the turn and the river). They elect to go with an all-in bet of their remaining £300.

   If position 5 calls, this will end the betting and force an early showdown because position 3 is all-in. However, if position 5 folds, position 3 will win without the need for the remaining community cards.

2   What decision should position 5 make? Although they have been doing okay, they went for a big bet when raising the stakes pre-flop. Also, an Ace has appeared in the flop. The player in this position will now be thinking that their remaining opponent may well have a pair of Aces, given that they called the original raise and then went all-in. To see whether position 3 is for real or is bluffing will cost position 5 £300. Yes, they still have their King, Jack and there is an Ace on the board, but the turn and river will have to be kind to leave them with a straight.

Very much aware that if they call for the £300 and then lose, the hand will have cost them £500. Position 5 folds.

   This meant that position 3 successfully executed a bluff, and took a pot of £715 as their reward. Of course, that £715 contained £500 which position 3 actually contributed to it, but at least the profit will have covered their blinds for a few more hands.

   What should be learned from this bluff is that position 3 decided to execute it not on the strength of their hand, but on the back of how they only had position 5 left in against them. It was a brave move, given the raise that position 5 had already made, but position 3 could well have reasoned that the raise was a bluff in itself. They may have also reasoned that position 5 had made their play on the hand very early and would therefore not want to commit much more to the pot.

With that example of a bluff in action – albeit a fairly adventurous one – let's move on and examine online tells. We didn't spend long looking at bluffing because, although it does have a part to play in internet poker, it is not as important as it is in real-life games, where the reaction of the other players can be much better judged. To add to this, for newcomers the best way to play poker, online or real-life, is to play the right hands in an aggressive enough way to frighten off some opponents, but not so aggressively that the pot is prevented from bubbling along until the showdown. Always remember that, in the end, the best hand left in will scoop the money.

Online Tells

Although we haven't spent that much time with bluffing, it is worth spending longer with the topic of online tells. Bluffing is a matter of choice, but online tells are not. In other words, a player chooses whether they want to execute a bluff, perhaps to boost a poor hand or possibly to disguise a good one. But a player could **unknowingly** give themselves away on a good hand through an online tell, and that could cost them chips. Equally so, if a player is unaware that an opponent is unwittingly giving out clues, they could be missing a profitable opportunity.

For anyone who remains unconvinced, consider this very old poker saying which originates from real-life games:

'If after sitting down at a poker table you can't spot the sucker within ten minutes, the sucker is probably you.'

This is a great way of remembering that playing poker is not only about watching the actions of the other players; it is also about being aware that the good ones will be watching you!

What is a Tell?

Putting it as basically as possible, with real-life games a tell is when a player inadvertently does something to indicate that their hand is either good or bad. Internet poker is just the same. In real-life games a nerve might twitch in a player's neck or they might start to fiddle with their chips more than they normally do.

Another real-life tell is how a player's eyes might widen when they first see a good hand developing. This is not easy to spot, but top-class poker players are very adept at doing so. Indeed, the best players in the world are frighteningly observant regarding what tells they can spot in their opponents. Fortunately, though, even the best players in the world cannot see anyone's eyes widen, or perhaps a nerve twitch in someone's neck, when playing online. But there are a few fairly obvious online tells and so newcomers should take note of them.

Taking Your Time

As you might expect, all sites place a maximum time limit which players must act within. A lot of sites give players 20–30 seconds to decide what to do, with a reminder being issued halfway through that time. When players exceed the given time, they will be 'timed out' and their hands folded. However, a lot of players fail to realise that the speed with which they act can be an online tell.

Many players react to their hole-cards in similar ways. If they feel good about their cards, they'll call, bet or raise very quickly. But if they are not sure, they will take a bit longer to decide. Good poker players, though, will adopt a policy of taking almost exactly the same amount of time to act no matter what the strength of their hand.

The amount of time they take will incorporate 'thinking time'. Therefore, they will allow themselves a few seconds to act on every hand, even if they intend to fold. This does take some control because the natural instinct with a bad hand is to fold it as soon as possible. But it is worth bearing in mind that the few extra seconds spent sitting there instead of immediately folding a bad hand will, in the long run, be rewarded many times over through other players never being able to read what you are holding.

As you watch other online players, you will need to develop a feel for whether they are delaying their actions because they simply always play that way, or if it is because they have a tough decision to make. Alternatively, they could be deliberately stalling (as it is called) as part of a bluff. This could well be the case if they have a really good hand, but are trying to make it look otherwise.

Their policy might be to take their time, hoping that their opponents will start to think they are debating whether to continue, when the truth is they are actually chomping at the bit to click the bet, raise or call button. Good notes may well help in these situations, but newcomers should also try to develop a 'feel' for what other players are doing anyway. However, the most important thing to remember is that most of the poor online players (fish) will probably have no idea about this kind of thing to begin with!

Incidentally, a really good way of taking the same amount of time to react whenever the game reaches you is the 'count to five' method. Simply become practised at counting five seconds off in your head (or longer if you think you'll need it). During whatever period you use, make your mind up over what you are going to do and then when that time is up hit the appropriate button. Generally speaking, between five and ten seconds should be enough time to decide your actions. This will not hold the game up too much either.

Pre-Action Buttons

You will recall that we discussed the pre-action buttons in an earlier chapter. Because of this we will not go over them again now, short of saying how they can be the biggest online tell of the lot. Always remember that using the pre-action buttons during the course of a hand can sometimes give an observant opponent a clue about the strength of the cards being held.

Of course, players should always also be aware of when an opponent appears to have used a pre-action button themselves. They might be doing so deliberately because they have a weak hand and are trying to bluff their opponents into thinking they have the opposite. But more often than not it is just be a mistake on their part.

Before we move away from pre-action buttons, what follows is an example illustrating how using one of them in particular can give the game away.

Imagine that you are sitting in the second-to-last betting position holding a pair of 7s. The flop comes as Ace, King, 10. Three other players remain in, including the one betting after you. One of the pre-action buttons available will be **Check / Fold** (clicking this means that if both of those sitting in an earlier position check, you check as well, but if anyone bets, you fold).

Knowing your hand is poor, you select this button hoping to take a free look at the betting action. But when it stops being free you want to fold. However, supposing the opponent behind you also plans to check, but doesn't use their pre-action button?

Those required to act before you check and, courtesy of the pre-action button, so do you. But through hitting that button straight away, especially if you usually count to five, your action will have been noticeably faster than normal. Therefore, if the opponent behind you picks up on this they will know that you probably used the **Check / Fold** pre-action button (as they will about any of the other players who have done the same thing). The conclusion they might well draw is that you are not very comfortable with your hand and are looking to ditch it.

Hence, they will realise that if they then execute a bluffing bet it is extremely likely you will fold. It would only take the other two players to also fold (remember, these two have already checked, which might suggest weakness) and the player behind you will have pinched a hand on the back of your online tell. So what, you may think, let them have it. But the chips they win in this hand might be the chips which help beat you in a later hand.

Again, this might seem trivial, but lots of trivial things added together often make something more substantial. Always remember that poker is a game of uncertainty based upon gathering as much knowledge as you can. The more you know, the more often you will win. Eliminate uncertainties and you'll add to your knowledge.

Aside from what we have already looked at, the manner in which players actually behave during a game can tell you plenty about their overall approach, and even their attitude. We examine examples of this now.

Can't Fold, Won't Fold

To begin with, look out for the players who very rarely fold. Players who inevitably call no matter how poor their cards, are generally loose, or simply don't know how to play the game. Or it may not even be one of those two things. Their reluctance to fold might arise simply because they like playing and thus find it hard to sit tight waiting for the good hands. Whatever it is, your task will be to punish their inability or unwillingness to fold by playing your good hands to the full. Really, this is another form of online tell.

Doubling Up

Some players take part in more than one game at the same time. This is a big error and observant opponents will note the players who do such a thing. Anyone who plays more than one game at one time is telling their opponents that they find it hard to sit patiently playing online poker the way in which it needs to be played. Think about it for a moment. Someone who is diving between games may well find concentration difficult. It will also suggest that they are not taking notes about their opponents because playing two games at once is hardly conducive to that.

In the end, anybody playing more than one game at the same time will probably allow their restlessness – make no mistake, that's what it is – to drive them into playing hands which should be left well alone. That is when a good player will be ready to step in. But how do you know someone is playing in two games at the same time? Easy, look at the lists in the lobby. Do this before you enter a game and then keep checking throughout whichever one you eventually choose to sit in on. A great way of exploiting a 'double-dipper', as those in the US call them, is to watch for when they go on tilt, despite not having had that bad a time in the game they share with you. Chances are they will have taken a beating elsewhere and be reacting to it on your table.

Size Matters

We examined buying into a game when we looked at money management. The only thing to add here is that the size of someone's pile of chips can be an online tell. If someone has a small pile of chips they have either bought into the game with a shorter amount than is usual, which suggests timidity, or they have been taking a beating. Whichever it is, on display here is some free information to be possibly taken advantage of should the opportunity arise.

Showing Off

Another topic which occasionally provokes debate between poker experts is whether you should show the cards to your opponents after you have pulled off a bluff. The general consensus is that it can do no harm, providing it is done in moderation: if you continually show yourself to have been bluffing, you are eventually going to be taken on and soundly thrashed!

Other than for 'advertising' purposes, and then not very often, showing your cards at the end of a hand is to be discouraged. Remember, poker is a game of uncertainties and is all about acquiring knowledge. Do not make the mistake of giving your opponents knowledge about the way you played your hand through revealing your cards – unless perhaps you are trying to set them up for a kill for a later hand.

Supposing you are in a late position, have a good hand, and are the first in the game to make a raise; should you go on to win fairly easily it might be an idea to show your cards. Further down the line when you are again in a late betting position, you might be able to steal a pot by playing a poor hand in the same way. If that works, why not show your cards again? The more observant players at your table will become puzzled about what type of game you are playing.

Generally, though, don't show your cards at the end of a hand. It's free information for your opponents.

That's about it with regard to online tells. There can be no doubt that there are quite a few of them. What is more, because the internet version of poker is much younger than its real-life counterpart, it is quite possible that not all tells have been discovered yet! Indeed, as the software that runs online poker sites becomes increasingly sophisticated, new tells will probably spring up. Therefore, in the notes you will eventually keep about the players you play against and the games you play in, make sure you leave enough space for writing down any fresh online tells which you may discover.

Note-Taking

As you might expect, our friends in the US have invented their own name for the business of taking notes about your online poker opponents. They call it 'having book'. Not to be confused with making a book (as a bookmaker would do), having book simply means collecting, sorting and then using information about the way other online players actually play. To avoid confusion we will continue to refer to this as note-taking rather than having book, but at least now you will know what the term means if you ever encounter it on a site somewhere.

So, you may ask, why do we need to take notes about the people we are playing against? The answer lies within the fact that poker is a game where there are a lot of unknowns. Hence, the more unknowns a player can eliminate, the better their chances of success. This is where note-taking enters the equation. Through keeping notes about how their opponents perform, players can eliminate some of the unknowns, and therefore increase their chances of winning. Here is an example:

Let us suppose that you are holding these hole-cards

The flop produces

After the flop it is just you and one opponent left in. Your opponent then makes a bet. Although you believe you have the best hand with your pair of Kings, you are not sure. The reason you cannot be sure is because you simply don't know what your opponent has bet with. Do they now have three 6s, or perhaps three 3s? Alternatively, perhaps they have got a pair of Kings with a high kicker, or perhaps a pair of 6s, or even just a pair of 3s. You just don't know.

It is precisely these situations that cause a number of experienced real-life poker players to shun the internet version of the game. Their argument is that in real life they might be able to pick up a tell from their opponent. But with online poker it is not as easy. However, if a player has been taking notes they have a weapon which is probably equally as powerful as the skill of being able to read their opponents.

In our example, providing that from either the current game or from previous encounters you have some notes on your remaining opponent, you will have a good chance of working out how that opponent usually plays hands like this. These notes may well carry the observation that your opponent frequently likes to play a big pair with a medium or poor kicker. Because you have a pair of Kings with a Queen kicker, you might now know where the advantage lies. Therefore, you may decide that your opponent is probably chancing their arm and so consequently elect to go for a raise.

After this your opponent may take you through to a showdown. However, in the showdown you could well find that your opponent had a pair of Kings with a 7 kicker. If that was the case, you'd take the pot, courtesy of your notes. Of course, without the notes you may have still made the right choice anyway, but the value they added to your game is obvious.

At various points in this book it has been pointed out that many players are keen to defend their blind bets. Having good notes on other players can be of great help here. For example, a detailed set of notes may show whether a player likes to raise, or even re-raise, from a blind position because they cannot bear to leave their blind (especially the big one) undefended.

Notes can be a great help in other areas as well. Here are another two examples.

You might be playing a game when an opponent you know logs in. In your consolidated notes it can be seen that this opponent has only ever raised three times in the considerable number of games they have shared with you. All three times they had a pair of Aces in the hole. A few hands after logging into the current game, they make a raise. So, you would be quite entitled to assume they must again be sitting on pocket Aces. Because you have considerably less than a pair of Aces, you decide it's wise to fold.

A further example could be if you are up against an opponent who has raised into a flop of Ace, King, King. The flop looks pretty frightening, carrying with it the possibility that your opponent is now sitting on a big hand. But your notes may well tell you that this opponent frequently bets into good-looking flops because they enjoy trying to steal pots through a pre-turn-card bluff. Furthermore, your notes also indicate that this opponent usually folds when faced with a re-raise. Hence, you can then play the hand not only on the back of what you hold, but also through knowing how this particular opponent is likely to behave.

These are just some quick examples of how note-taking can be an enormous help. But although their value can easily be seen, you might still be wondering, 'Am I ever going to come up against the same opponents frequently enough to make it worthwhile?' This question can be answered in three ways.

First, the best online poker players all keep notes and if you start to become a serious and successful opponent they will soon have notes on you. Second, although your notes might only lead you to profit from one or two hands per session, that is still a decent return, given how the notes will have cost nothing to compile. Third, notes can be of great benefit even in the short term. For example, it might be that you end up playing in the same game for three hours. During that time a couple of your opponents might stay with you. If you have been playing selective / aggressive, you should definitely have had the time to take notes about those players. Subsequently, a hand might come along where the notes enable you to pick up a decent pot.

By now you are, hopefully, convinced regarding note-taking – but how do you do it effectively?

Basic Notes

It is best to start off your note-taking with just the basics. These will only be a simple record of when each player enters a game and how much money they buy in with. Keeping the notes can be done on your PC (a lot of poker sites actually offer this facility) or through having a notebook and pen to hand. Let's suppose that you decide to use a notebook.

It is best to lay the book out so that each player is given two facing pages (for clarity). When entering a game, create an entry for each player already taking part and then simply add pages for every new player that comes in afterwards. The result of this should look something like the following:

> LeapingLen from Liverpool
> 11/02/05, 21.50hrs
> £2–£4 hold 'em, £100

This shows that LeapingLen from Liverpool joined the £2 / £4 Texas Hold 'em game with a buy-in of £100 at ten minutes to ten on the evening of 11 February 2005. Of course, it may not always be possible to collect information about where a player comes from. This will depend upon how they have set up their on-screen ID. In this instance, though, the fact that Len has said he is from Liverpool will be of no help to anyone playing in the UK.

But if he had been from, say, Los Angeles, you would know he was playing at ten minutes to two in the afternoon. This might suggest he was having a quick game in his lunch hour (and thus might be anxious to see some action because of limited time), or it could mean he is a night worker who has just got up (and therefore might still be tired). Naturally, it might not mean either of these two things, but there would be no harm in keeping an eye on his play to see if he was 'chip happy'. Again, it is free information which there is no downside to collecting.

Having written down the basic information, you might then extend the note like this:

> LeapingLen from Liverpool
> 11/02/05, 21.50hrs
> £2–£4 hold 'em, £100
> Left game at 23.15hrs, lost £45

Here you have just recorded that LeapingLen quit the game at 23.15 having suffered a loss of £45. Of course, it could have been that the information about his loss was impossible to record because he left the game when you were not paying attention. The only way of overcoming these situations is to keep your eyes on the screen as much as you can. It is also worth remembering that to know what he had lost you would have needed to be keeping a running record of his chip size. This is not a difficult task though; simply jot it down just before each new deal.

In the early days, records like this don't have to be incredibly detailed. At this stage it is much more about being able to develop a general picture of your opponents ready for possible future use. Using LeapingLen as an example again, let's look at how even the most basic information can be of assistance:

LeapingLen from Liverpool
11/02/05, 21.50hrs
£2–£4 hold 'em, £100
Left game at 23.15hrs, lost £45
★★★★

LeapingLen from Liverpool
16/02/05, 22.30hrs
£2–£4 hold 'em, £100
Left game at 23.32hrs, lost £36
★★★★

LeapingLen from Liverpool
18/02/05, 22.15hrs
£2–£4 hold 'em, £80 (short buy-in?)
Left game at 23.40hrs, lost £17
★★★★

LeapingLen from Liverpool
21/02/05, 21.30hrs
£2–£4 hold 'em, £70
Missed leaving but short buy-in?
★★★★

LeapingLen from Liverpool
28/02/05, 22.37hrs
£2–£4 hold 'em, £120
Left game at 23.05hrs, lost £48
★★★★

Not much detective work would be required to see that LeapingLen did not have a very good 18 days (from 11 to 28 February) playing Texas Hold 'em. Perhaps he just hit an unlucky spell, but it could be that he is simply a poor player. If it is the latter, this is information worth bearing in mind for any possible future occasion when you might end up in a showdown with him.

You will also have seen the notes concerning his two possible short buy-ins. This could tell you that because he then came back with his more usual buy-in on 28 February he had perhaps started to run short of money before eventually receiving his salary at month end. But how could this information be of assistance in the future? Simple: next time he makes a short buy-in, it could be a sign that he will have to play cautiously, and you thus may be able to bully him out of a pot or two through calling a bluff.

More Sophisticated Notes

You will have seen from the previous couple of pages that note-taking is not that difficult. Bearing this in mind then, why not extend it further? The suggestion was to keep a double page free in your notebook for each player. This was for clarity purposes. On the left-hand side of the book keep the information already discussed, but on the right-hand side you could record consolidated information. Look at the following example.

LeapingLen from Liverpool 11/02/05, 21.50hrs £2–£4 hold 'em, £100 Left game at 23.15hrs, lost £45 ★★★★	LeapingLen from Liverpool Plays blinds more often than not
LeapingLen form Liverpool 16/02/05, 22.30hrs £2–£4 hold 'em, £100 Left game at 23.32hrs, lost £36 ★★★★	Tends to show cards after a bluff Almost always folds when facing a re-raise
LeapingLen from Liverpool 18/02/05, 22.15hrs £2–£4 hold 'em, £80 (short buy-in?) Left game at 23.40hrs, lost £17 ★★★★	Rarely raises from early position Hole-cards seen played by him Ace King, Ace Queen, King Queen, Pair K's, Pair 9's
LeapingLen from Liverpool 21/02/05, 21.30hrs £2–£4 hold 'em, £70 Missed leaving but short buy-in? ★★★★	Leaves game when losing, weak player ... not a threat

By extending your notes in this way, you can really begin to develop pen-pictures of other players. Clearly, LeapingLen is no great shakes and someone who appears to be quite a timid player. He usually defends his blinds, but rarely raises from an early position. From that information it is hard not to form the view that LeapingLen only likes to play high hole-cards, which is good, but overall appears to be rather a weak player who does not generally pose a threat.

Any player who combines notes like these with a close scrutiny of their opponents will soon be a long way in front of the vast majority of other online players. This is because a very high number of online poker players think it is too much like hard work. They need to think again.

Online poker has become hugely popular because it is an easy method of gambling. You don't have to leave the comfort of your own home and it is a very anonymous way of having a bet. But, if it is that easy, why doesn't everyone win? Well, quite simply, not everyone **can** win. It would be impossible for everyone to do so because players are playing one another, not the site operator (except for the rake). Sadly, most players actually lose at online poker, but those that buck the trend are the ones who **do not** think making money from online poker is easy. They are the ones who realise that there are very few shortcuts in life and that to be successful in almost any field takes hard work. Online poker is no different. The players that win regularly are the ones who put in the work through showing discipline, playing selectively / aggressively, managing their stakes, and **taking notes**. At first it will seem hard, but you will need to get into the habit of doing so. Once it becomes habit, you will be surprised how easy it is.

All About You

Of course, there is one player you can keep the most incredibly detailed notes about. That player is you. Not to keep notes on your own play is unforgivable. Obviously, there will be no need to keep notes about what type of player you are because you should find that out pretty quickly, but you should keep notes about the hands you play, possibly why you played them and, as we said earlier when looking at money-management, your profit and loss figures.

As well as all this you should keep track of the times you defended your blinds, when you raised, when you folded, and what positions you did best and worst from. This is all quite easy through use of the software that a number of top sites provide which will record this very information. The work for the player will be in the analysis. Most serious online poker players say the same thing: once they started to keep notes and records about their own play, they began to make more money. Through analysing the notes on themselves, they were able to see their strengths and weaknesses much easier. It will be the same for you.

Further Information

When the idea for this book was first devised, it was the intention to create a final chapter in which all the major internet poker sites were closely examined. However, the online poker world moves quickly and it has become clear that such a chapter would not be of any real value. Quite honestly, internet poker has become so popular that most of the sites now have very similar formats. Indeed, a number of sites are using software developed by the same company and so they look, except for their branding, almost identical. Yes, there are exceptions such as True Poker, which has a brilliant set of graphics (worth visiting for that alone), but even they have the same basic format when it comes to the lobby, menu options, game lists and information buttons.

Therefore, later on in this final chapter we will take a brief look at a cross-section of the top online poker sites. In doing so, we will list a few details about each, with the most important thing being the level of competition newcomers can expect to find on them!

But to begin, what follows is an extensive glossary of online poker terms. After that you will find a selection of further reading, plus some websites of poker interest.

Glossary of Online Poker Terms

Action: The betting in a game. This term also encompasses the opportunity to bet. Hence, if you are playing a game and another player uses the chat box to say 'the action here is very hot', they would mean the betting in the game was quite intense. However, when it is your turn to call, bet, raise, check or fold, the action is said to rest with you.

All-in: The term used to describe when a player bets all of their remaining chips. Through doing so, they will ensure their place in any showdown. Remember though, following an all-in, the betting must still be equalised. Once the betting has been equalised, any further action among the remaining players will take place in a side pot.

All-in is also a term used when a player becomes disconnected from an online game. They will then only be eligible to win what was in the pot up to the point they became disconnected. This is generally known as an 'all-in disconnect'.

Antes: In some forms of poker, compulsory bets which each player must make before the cards are dealt. In Texas Hold 'em the equivalent is the **blinds**.

Avatar: A computer-generated character used to represent a player in an online game.

B & M: A term often used in online poker to describe a real-life card room, usually meaning a casino. It is short for bricks and mortar.

Back Door: The term used when a straight (flush or not) is completed only with the turn and river cards.

Bad Beat: A bad beat is when a player loses a showdown that they were the statistical favourite for.

Bankroll: A term often used to describe the amount of money a player makes available to play poker with. This might be for one session of playing, or for a specified period of time.

Blinds: The small blind and the big blind are the compulsory bets made at the start of each new hand. The big blind is generally an increased multiple of the small blind. The requirement to post blinds revolves around the table in front of the deal; in other words, the two players to the immediate left of the dealer will be responsible for making the blind bets – small blind first, large blind second.

Board: The name given to the community cards. Also, a term sometimes used to describe the waiting list for a game.

Bust (as in **Busted**): The term used to describe a player losing all of their chips; or even worse, their entire bankroll!

Button: A term used to describe the marker which tells the players who the dealer is. Also known as the disc.

Buy-in: The amount of chips that a player enters the game with, or the cost of entering into a tournament.

Call: This is when a player matches the bet made by the previous player.

Capped: The term used to describe a game in which there are a maximum number of raises allowed. Obviously, this is a term unique to fixed-limit or pot-limit games. When a game is said to be capped, the maximum number of raises will have been reached.

Chat Box: The term used to describe a window available on the game screens of all online poker sites, which can be used by the players to talk to one another via text.

Check: The term used to describe when a player wants to continue in the betting but does not want to make a bet at that immediate point. Checks are only allowed until a real bet is actually made.

Check / Fold: This option, available only with internet poker through a pre-action button, allows a player to check their hand if possible, but if not – because a bet has been made before the action comes to them – to fold instead.

Check-Raise: The same as **Check / Fold** apart from the fact that the player using this option is saying they will check if possible, but if not will make a raise.

Community Cards: Another name given to the face-up cards dealt in the middle of the table and shared by all the players.

Connected (or **Connectors**): When hole-cards are of consecutive value.

Cracked: The term used to describe when hole-cards of two Aces end up being beaten. Hence, the Aces have been 'cracked'.

Deuce: The 2 card.

Down-Cards: A less common term for **hole-cards**.

Draw Hand: The term used when a hand needs certain community cards to appear for it to win. For example, if a player's hole-cards are J ♠, 10 ♠ and the flop comes out as 8 ♠, 9 ♠, A ♥ the player would then have a good drawing hand. This is because either the 7 ♠ or Q ♠ on the turn or the river would give them a straight flush. If the same two value cards came out, but either both or only one was not a spade, they would still have a straight. Lastly, if any spade except the Queen or 7 came out the player would still have a flush.

Drawing Dead: This is the term used when there are still community cards to come, but none of them can improve a hand. In these cases the player with that hand is said to be drawing dead.

Fifth Street: The less common term for the river card.

Fish: A nickname that better players give to bad, losing players.

Flat Call: Where a player calls when a raise may have been more appropriate.

Flop: The first three community cards to be dealt.

Flush: A hand that contains five cards of the same suit.

Fold: The term used to describe when a player drops out of a hand. In these instances they fold their cards.

Fourth Street: The less common term for the turn card.

Freeroll: This is when a poker site offers a tournament which carries no entry fee, but does carry prize money.

Full House: A hand comprising three of a kind and a pair.

Gut Shot: A name given to a very unlikely draw, such as an inside straight.

Hand: A term that has two meanings: either the cards that form a player's holding, or a way of describing the action from deal to showdown.

Hand Log: The recorded history of every hand showing every action taken by each of the players. These can be found on most sites with a bit of clicking around!

Heads-up: The term used to describe when only two players are competing for a pot. (Many sites offer heads-up play as a facility.)

High Card: The highest ranking card in a hand that does not contain even a pair.

Hole-cards: The two face-down cards dealt to each player at the start of every hand.

Inside Straight: The term used to describe the situation when a set of cards has a gap which requires another card to fill it before a straight can be made. For example, if a player has 6, 7, 8 and the flop and turn cards have produced 10, J, 2, 2, that player needs a 9 to come out on the river to complete their straight.

Kicker: The name given to the card that is used to break a tie between hands of the same value. Hence, if two players both have a pair of Aces, the one with the next highest card in their five would win.

Limping: A term used to describe when a player calls the big blind in the pre-flop betting.

List: The term used to describe the place where the names of any players waiting to enter a game can be found.

Lobby: The first screen that players encounter when they log on to an online poker site.

Loose Play / Loose Player: When players, or just one player on their own, continues to bet in defiance of unfavourable odds about them completing their hands.

Main Pot: The term used to describe the principal amount of money being competed for. After an all-in, any further betting goes into a side pot.

Monkeyfish: A term used to describe a loose player who also does not appear to know how to play poker.

Muck: Has two meanings, one as a noun and one as a verb. The muck pile is the name given to the pile of cards that has been folded. But to muck your cards means to return them to the muck pile – in other words, to fold.

Multi-table Tournament: The term used to describe a tournament where players are competing at more than one table. As players are eliminated, the number of tables will decrease until there is just one left. On that final table the last player left in will be the tournament winner.

No-Limit: Where the only restriction on each bet is the number of chips the player making it has in play.

Nuts: The term used to describe the very best combination of cards currently available. Obviously, the nuts on the flop might not be the nuts after the turn or the river. As stated in an earlier chapter, whenever you stay in the betting to the flop and beyond always work out what the nut hand could be.

On Tilt: The term used to describe when a player loses control of their betting and starts to behave irrationally.

Online Tells: Patterns of behaviour demonstrated by players which give away the strength, or weakness, of their hand.

Open-ended Straight: A holding of four cards where a fifth card at either end would complete a straight (flush or not). Hence, if a player holds 8, 9 and the flop has produced 7, 10, K, the player needs either a 6 or a Jack to come out on the turn or the river to complete their straight.

Outs: The number of possibilities a player has to win a pot, based on the current standing of their cards. Hence, if a player holds a pair of Aces and believes three of them would be enough to win the hand, they have two outs because there are only two Aces theoretically still available. It is theoretical because another player might already hold one or both of the Aces, which would reduce or eliminate the number of outs. However, in poker what other players might hold is not taken into account when it comes to calculating outs.

Over Card(s): The term used when a set of hole-cards is of higher value than the community cards on the board. For example, a player holding a pair of Aces has a higher-value hand if the flop has come out 10, 7, 6.

Pass: A term sometimes used, especially in the US, to describe when a player folds their cards. In some places it is also used to describe when a player checks.

Play-chips: The term used to describe the chips in play-money games.

Playing the Board: This is when a player uses all five community cards as their hand.

Pocket Pair: Used to describe when a player's hole-cards are a pair.

Pocket Rockets: A pair of Aces as hole-cards.

Position: The place at the table each player holds in relation to the dealer.

Pot: The total of the money bet in any one hand.

Pot-Limit: The term used to describe a game where the amount of each bet is restricted to the amount of money already in the pot, but only after what it would cost to call the last bet is taken into account.

Raise: When a player bets more into the pot than the previous player did.

Re-buy: This is the act of obtaining more chips during a game. However, this is not allowed during the course of a hand.

Re-raise: When a player raises immediately after the player before them has done so.

Ring Games: The name given to non-tournament games.

River: The fifth and final community card.

Royal Flush: The term used to describe the very best possible hand in poker. It comprises an Ace, King, Queen, Jack and 10 of the same suit.

Set (as in '**a set**'): The term used to describe when a pocket pair connects with one of the community cards to make three of a kind.

Sharks: The nickname given to players who win consistently; those who eat up the fish.

Showdown: The final act of each deal which takes place after all the betting is complete. The players that remain in the game then show their cards, with the highest hand winning the pot (or lowest hand if hi / lo is being played).

Side Pot: The term used to describe the sum of money being played for if any betting action takes place after one or more players have gone all-in. In other words, the side pot is available to all those players who are not all-in. Incidentally, it is possible to have more than one side pot if any of the players go all-in when contesting a side pot from earlier in the hand.

Split Pot: This is when two or more players have exactly the same value hands. Hence, the pot will be divided between them.

Stack: Possibly now a slightly old-fashioned term for the amount of chips each player has in play. Derived from real-life games, this term is not so relevant with internet poker.

Starting Hand: The two face-down hole-cards dealt to each player.

Straight: The term used to describe a hand of consecutive value cards where the suit does not count. Hence, 2, 3, 4, 5, 6 comprising different suited cards is said to be a '6-high straight'.

Straight Flush: The same as a straight, but where the cards are of the same suit. A straight flush is more valuable than a straight.

Table Stakes: A player's table stakes is the amount of money they have on the table at any one time. It is also the maximum amount that a player can lose on any one hand, due to the fact that if another bet exceeds that amount the player can either fold or go all-in.

Trap: Where a player bets sparingly, or perhaps even checks, when they have a really good hand. The aim of this is to suck other players into betting. Once that is achieved, the first player then raises. Setting a trap is most commonly done after the turn card but before the river.

Trey: The 3 card.

Trips: A term used to describe three cards of the same type – for example, three Aces or three 2s.

Turn: The most commonly used term for the fourth community card.

Under the Gun: The term used for describing the table position occupied by the first player to act in each betting round.

Wheel: A term used to describe the lowest possible straight – Ace, 2, 3, 4, 5.

That's a comprehensive look at online poker terms. Now, let's have a quick look at the different hand nicknames.

Pairs

Aces: Pocket Rockets, Bullets or American Airlines

Kings: Cowboys or King Kong

Queens: Double Date, Canadian Aces, Siegfried and Roy

Jacks: Fish Hooks

Tens: Railroad Tracks

Nines: German Virgin ('nein, nein' – think about it!)

Eights: Snowmen

Sevens: Sunset Strip

Sixes: Route 66

Fives: Speed Limit (obviously of US origin)

Fours: Magnum or Sail Boat

Threes: Crabs

Twos: Ducks

Other Hands

Ace / King: Big Slick

Ace / Queen: Big Chick

Ace / Jack: Black Jack or Jack-ass

King / Queen: Royalty or Marriage

King / Jack: Kojak

Jack / Five: Jackson Five

Queen / Three: Gay Waiter

Nine / Five: Dolly Parton

Ace / Eight: Dead Man's Hand

King / Nine: Canine

Jack / Four: Flat Tyre

Moving on, here's a very brief look at the abbreviations used when players chat to each other during the course of a game.

m8 = mate

nh = nice hand, used to tell another player when they had a good hand

vnh = very nice hand, a further compliment to nice hand

gg = good going, used when a player wins a big hand

lol = laugh out loud, used to tell another player you found something they said was amusing

ty = thank you, used in reaction to nh or vnh

wtf = what the f***?, self-explanatory!

st8 = straight, used to describe a straight

wp = well played, used to congratulate another player when they played a hand well – perhaps having executed a bluff or kept other players in the betting when they had a really strong hand

A Selection of Online Poker Sites

Most poker sites use US dollars, so we have quoted dollar amounts below. Incidentally, if you are using pounds sterling, the sites convert to dollars automatically.

www.betfairpoker.com

This site is owned and operated by the betting exchange people, Betfair. It's a reasonable site although a lot of the players on it know what they are doing and so the competition is quite tough.

www.coralpoker.com

This is a UK bookmaker-owned site. There is nothing special to report here. The competition is weak to fair at the lower-level games.

www.empirepoker.com

This is one of the larger sites. At peak times over 15,000 players contest their real-money games. There are nice graphics which are easy on the eye, although the games can be a bit slow. With so many players logged on, there is plenty of opportunity to find fish, but then there are also plenty of sharks swimming around as well.

There are usually plenty of bonuses on offer so check that out when you look at the site.

Plenty of tournaments are available and note that this site also hosts daily and monthly free-entry events. One of them carries prize money of $5000. Also look out for their VIP club which awards points to players who play regularly.

EmpirePoker only displays the average pot size in the ring games, which is a surprise for such a big site. Overall, it is not the best site when it comes to providing information about its games.

At EmpirePoker the minimum deposit is $50. It is strongly recommended for beginners.

www.ladbrokespoker.com

Probably the premier European-based poker site, this site is run by the UK's leading bookmaker, Ladbrokes. Part of the Hilton Group, Ladbrokes offers a huge range of games on their poker site and on one Sunday night early in January 2006 they could boast of having 6622 players connected with 3742 actually seated in games!

The site offers a large number of tournaments, many of them free to enter, some of which carry fantastic prizes for the winners.

This is a colourful site with plenty of information (the screen shots in this book come from here) and one that both welcomes and easily accommodates every range of player, from beginner to expert.

It's well worth a visit and a recommended starting point for novices.

www.littlewoodspoker.com

This is quite a busy site. Most of the time there is a lot of activity across a fair selection of games. At the time of writing, it was undergoing a major publicity exercise.

www.pacificpoker.com

This is often said to be the site where the worst players on the internet find a home. Limits at Pacific range from 5–10 cents through to $30–60. This is a site where the very low-limit games see tremendous amounts of activity. It is a great site for beginners, or for anyone who doesn't want to risk much cash.

The software at Pacific is pretty slow but for a beginner that is an advantage, as it will afford more thinking time.

At the time of writing, Pacific was offering a bonus of 25 per cent on first-time deposits (maximum bonus $100). Also, for every $10 staked, one point is earned. For every 100 points accumulated, a bonus of $1 is awarded. On-screen, Pacific displays the flop percentage and the average pot.

The minimum deposit at Pacific is $20. This site is also highly recommended for newcomers because of the weakness of the other players.

www.paradisepoker.com

This is one of the early sites which is now pretty static in terms of growth; it's certainly nothing like as big as PartyPoker or Ladbrokes. One of the reasons for this is the pretty tough competition you'll meet on the site.

It has fast software and good graphics. Bonuses need to be hunted down a bit, though. Paradise Poker displays flop percentage and average pot size.

The minimum deposit at Paradise Poker is $50. Overall, it's quite a good site, but one where beginners need to be very careful. This is a site you should definitely make a beeline for if you want to pay for an online poker education in terms of early losses!

www.partypoker.com

This site is now the biggest in the world and shares games with EmpirePoker. PartyPoker hosts a huge number of games but the competition is stiff, especially in the bigger-money games. It is still worth checking out for newcomers, though, because it does offer some good sign-up bonuses.

www.planetpoker.com

This was one of the original online poker sites. The competition has never been that tough and there are always lots of lower-limit games. The site is pretty good for the beginner, and the graphics, although not outstanding, are quite colourful if not that different from a few other sites.

www.pokerstars.com

This is a site for the better poker players where fish are soon gobbled up, not that many swim here to start with. Growing all the time, PokerStars hosts many multi-table tournaments. From the mid-staking games upwards, the standard of play is tough and so it is not a good place for complete beginners.

The software is fine and the graphics quite colourful. This is a site that does offer many bonuses. On-screen information is fair.

This is a reasonable site but tough for beginners. It's worth playing on to gain some real experience, but do so only for small stakes.

www.sportingoddspoker.com

In terms of winning money this site is the best! The graphics are boring and the software does not sprint, but the standard of play is often atrocious. For some reason, presumably because of where the owners promote it, this site attracts a huge number of hot-headed individuals from many parts of Europe and Africa. It is a new site and so no doubt the sharks are swimming to it as we speak, but it's a great site for beginners – if you have the nerve. Just check out their no-limit action!

www.truepoker.com

Home   About Us   Community   Promos   Refer a Friend   Affiliate Program   Contact Us   Help

Welcome to True Poker

Your most true-to-life Online Poker experience

This is probably the site with the best graphics in online poker, with highly detailed, 3-D images with animated characters. You'll love how each player's character makes an audio sound such as 'fold' or 'forget about it'. Competition here is reasonable to weak, mostly because it is a low-staking site.

Surprisingly this is still a relatively small site with a moderate choice of games. At the time of writing, only lower-stakes fixed-limit and no-limit Hold 'em games were played. There are not many tournaments. The pace of play at True Poker is pretty slow, so it's good for beginners. Bonuses are standard.

www.ultimatebet.com

This is quite a nice site but the competition here is considerably stiffer than at many of its rivals. The software and graphics are good, very colourful and actually quite relaxing.

Ultimatebet does offer bonuses, but they are not that attractive so don't be too concerned with them. This is another site that lists both the average pot and the average flop percentage.

This is a site where the low-limit games are probably okay for beginners, but where you can still be caught out by the sharks.

www.vcpoker.com

This is a site that does not accept players from the US; vcpoker is owned and run by Victor Chandler, an established UK bookmaker. There are lots of games here but no-limit Hold 'em seems to be especially popular. The competition is reasonable, but this is still not somewhere that beginners should expect an easy ride. The lack of US players makes this a site popular with those in the UK.

The graphics at Victor Chandler are interesting, to say the least. The cards are displayed much bigger than at other sites and the audio alarm to remind a player it is their turn would double up well as an alarm clock! Perhaps, though, the background to the tables should be made a bit lighter. The software appears very quick and the games flash through as a result.

This is a pretty good site for bonuses with, at the time of writing, 25 per cent up to a maximum of $100 available for first-time deposits. Be aware, though, these bonuses are not always for immediate cash. You will have to play a fair number of 'raked' hands first.

www.williamhill.co.uk

This is a relatively new poker site. It is owned and operated by the well-known UK bookmaking company William Hill.

A Selection of Further Online Poker Reading

Hold 'em for Advanced Players by David Sklansky and Mason Malmuth (published by Two Plus Two Publishing)

How Good is Your Pot-limit Hold 'em? by Stewart Reuben (published by D & B Publishing)

How to Play Poker by Peter Arnold (published by Hamlyn, a division of Octopus Publishing Group Ltd)

Internet Poker – How to Play and Beat Online Poker Games by Lou Krieger and Kathleen Keller Watterson (published by ConJelCo)

Killer Poker Online by John Vorhaus (published by Lyle Stuart, Kensington Publishing Corporation)

Middle Limit Hold 'em Poker by Bob Ciaffone and Jim Brier (published by Bob Ciaffone)

Poker for Dummies by Richard D Harroch and Lou Krieger (published by Hungry Minds)

Poker on the Internet by Andrew Kinsman (published by D & B Publishing)

Tournament Poker for Advanced Players by David Sklansky (published by Two Plus Two Publishing)

Winning Low-limit Hold 'em (2nd edition) by Lee Jones (published by ConJelCo)

A Selection of Online Poker Products

www.highstakes.co.uk

This is a UK-based online bookshop selling a vast range of gambling books, including the very latest poker titles.

www.playwinningpoker.com

This is a site offering tuition from a top-line professional poker player, Steve Badger.

www.pokercharts.com

This is a web-based application that enables players to analyse their long-run poker performance through entering the date, venue, game profit / loss and duration of each session they play. Pokercharts then works out the numbers and produces a range of statistics and graphs.

www.pokerschoolonline.com

This is another site offering tuition. Subscribers pay a monthly fee and in return receive access to audio lessons, articles, hand analysis, etc.

www.pokertracker.com

This is a Windows-based program allowing players to analyse their play. Again, it works with hand histories and, at the time of writing, supported data from Paradise Poker, PartyPoker and PokerStars. Free trial versions are available for download.

www.thsoftware.com

PokerStat is a statistical database program available on this site that allows players to analyse the strengths and weaknesses of their own play, and that of their opponents. To achieve this task, the software utilises online hand histories. At the time of writing, the product supported only Paradise Poker hand histories but there were plans to extend it to other sites.

www.wilsonsw.com

This is the leading poker simulation software company, with different programs for Texas Hold 'em, Omaha, Seven-card Stud and others.

Miscellaneous Sites of Poker Interest

www.chanpoker.com

This is the official site of Johnny Chan, winner of six World Series of Poker titles. It's worth a quick look for the RealPlayer videos on tournament play.

www.philhellmuth.com

This is the personal site of Phil Hellmuth, one of the world's top poker players, who has won multiple World Series of Poker titles.

www.pokah.com

This is an online poker forum.

www.pokertips.org

This is an excellent site with lots of poker tips, all done in nice colours as well.

www.pokertop10.com

This is a site listing 'poker top ten' lists – an excellent starting point for further research.

www.twodimes.net

This is a great site where you can calculate showdown odds for different Texas Hold 'em hands.

Index